POTTERVILLE MIDDLE SCHOOL

Your Health and You

YOUR

Lothrop, Lee & Shepard Co., Inc.

NEW YORK

POTTERVILLE MIDDLE SCHOOL

HEALTH and YOU

by Charles Gramet

ILLUSTRATED WITH DRAWINGS BY
Rey Abruzzi
AND WITH PHOTOGRAPHS

Copyright © 1968 by Charles Gramet
Library of Congress Catalog Card Number: 67-18034
Manufactured in the United States of America
All rights reserved

1   2   3   4   5   72   71   70   69   68

Photograph Credits

Page 30: The Great Atlantic & Pacific Tea Company. Page 96: Sonotone
Corporation. Page 135: Jones & Loughlin Steel Corporation. Page
136: The Great Atlantic & Pacific Tea Company. Page 137: National
Dairy Council. Page 138: U. S. Department of Agriculture. Page 141: U. S.
Fish & Wildlife Service. Page 142: Department of Water Supply,
Gas & Electricity, New York City, Division of Water Supply Control.
Page 143: Department of Water Supply, Gas & Electricity, New
York City, Division of Water Supply Control. Page 147: New York State
Department of Health, Air Pollution Control Board. Page 149: United
States Public Health Service. Page 155: Federal Security Agency.
Public Health Service.

This book is dedicated to my wife,
Dora Sivin Gramet. Her help in every aspect
of its preparation has been invaluable.
Her understanding of young people has been
a guide and an inspiration.

Contents

Introduction

When all goes well in your body you are not aware of any part of it. That is as it should be. That is good health. But sometimes you may feel an ache or a pain in one part of the body or another. Then you may become aware of a tooth, or your throat, or your stomach. That part of your body would not be working well; it would be in poor health.

This book will help you to understand your body. You will learn how your body is organized, the role each part plays in the organization; and what you can do to keep all the parts working well.

The science of medicine has made it possible for doctors to prevent many diseases and, most often, to restore your health when illnesses or accidents occur. Hygiene, the science of health, tells you how, by caring for your body, you can do your part to make and keep it healthier. The two sciences assure you of a longer, happier, healthier life.

:one:
Your body is an organization

Look at yourself in a full-length mirror to see the general plan of structure of your body.

The greater part is the trunk, extending from the neck to the hips. The upper part of the trunk is the chest; the lower part is the abdomen. The trunk houses most of the "vital" organs, so called because their work is vital in keeping the body alive.

The neck connects the trunk with the head, which houses and protects one of our most sensitive vital organs—the brain. The openings in the head enable you to take in food, fluids, oxygen, and other materials that your body needs for work and play, for growth and repair. Through these openings some of the body wastes are given off. In the head, too, are the principal sense organs—the nose, eyes, ears, and tongue, which help you to learn what is going on about you and to enjoy your everyday environment.

Attached to the trunk are two pairs of limbs—the arms at the shoulders, the legs at the hips. The limbs are not vital, although they may seem so to you; but they are very useful.

Knowledge of the location, the structure, and the function of each of the vital organs, and of the relation of each to all others, was accumulated over many hundreds of years. Doctors, operating on animal and human bodies with such tools and under such conditions as then existed, passed on what they learned about the human body. In this way, the science of human anatomy gradually developed. This is the science that studies the size, shape, position, organization, and interrelation of the parts of the body. The organs have now been described very accurately and in great detail, and the organization of the human body is no longer the great mystery that it once was.

A tremendous advance in the knowledge of human anatomy resulted from the invention of the light microscope in the early part of the seventeenth century. Light microscopes use glass lenses and light rays to enlarge, or magnify, very tiny objects as many as two thousand times.

Electron microscopes have been invented recently that use beams of electrons instead of light rays, and use electromagnetic, instead of glass, lenses. These powerful electron microscopes can enlarge a tiny object as many as 200,000 times.

The microscope has been an invaluable aid to scientists studying the tiny units, called cells, of every organ in the body.

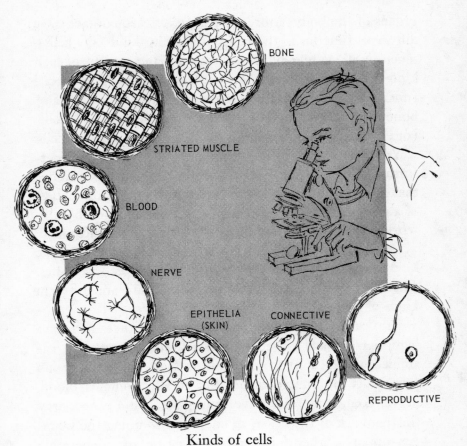

Kinds of cells

It has been estimated that each human body is made up of very many trillions of cells. Every cell in every organ has the same basic structure. Within each is a dense, ball-shaped part called the nucleus, surrounded by a less dense material called the cytoplasm. The entire cell is enclosed in a very thin skin, or membrane.

Cells are the units of work and of organization of the

organs of the body. Moreover, since different organs have different functions, there are different kinds of cells—seven in all. While all have the same basic structure, each kind has special features that enable it to perform its special function. The seven kinds, shown in the illustration, are: bone cells, muscle cells, blood cells, nerve cells, epithelial (or covering) cells, connective cells and reproductive cells.

You may wonder how each cell is directed in the performance of its special job. There is convincing evidence that a single substance in the nucleus (the control center) of each cell is solely responsible for directing each cell's work. Called DNA for short, it is deoxyribonucleic acid.

Cells do not work independently. Many of the same kind work together in cooperating groups called tissues. There are as many kinds of tissues as there are different kinds of cells.

Tissues do not work independently either. When a section from any organ (the heart, for example) is examined under a microscope, it is seen to be made up principally of muscle tissue. But it also contains blood, nerve, connective, and covering tissues. All are necessary for the work of the heart; all cooperate in doing the work. An organ is, therefore, an organization of cooperating tissues.

Nor do organs work independently. The brain, the heart, the lungs, the stomach, and other organs have important roles, but they function only in cooperation with other organs. Each of the major functions of your body is performed by a group of cooperating organs known as a system.

Thus, scientists have discovered that your body is an organization made up first of cells, then of tissues, then of organs, and, finally, of systems. The systems, too, co-operate, and you are thereby able to function as a single, coordinated individual.

Medical doctors and scientists have learned much about the organs and how they work by the use of X-rays. Unlike light rays, the X-rays are able to pass through solid objects. They do so more readily through soft ones, like muscles, than through hard ones, like bones. The X-ray image, a shadow picture, may be viewed on a special screen or photographed on film. Such a picture enables a doctor to get information about the condition of a particular organ.

Since the bones are the hardest and the densest parts, an X-ray picture of the entire body will clearly show its bony framework, the skeleton. It is made up of 206 separate bones of different sizes and shapes.

The bones of the head make up the skull. They cannot be separated, for they are joined tightly to one another, except for the lower jaw, which can be moved. All other bones of the body are held together by ligaments, bands of very tough fibers of connective tissue that are firmly attached to the bones.

If you have ever turned an ankle, you know how ligaments act. They will turn and twist, but they will not stretch. The fibers are so tough that the bones to which ligaments are attached may break before the ligaments will

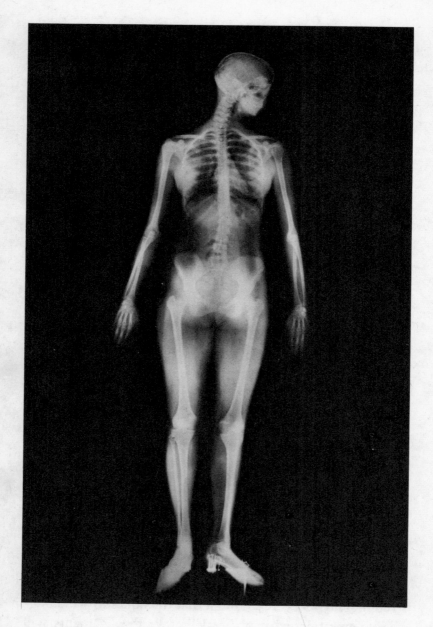

X-ray of body

tear. A ligament may be pulled or twisted so severely, however, that some of its fibers will snap. This results in a sprain. The more fibers that are torn, the more severe the sprain. The commonest ones are those of the ankle, but sprains of the wrist, fingers, knee, shoulder, back—even of the head-neck joint—are possible.

Although the bones are hard and rigid, the skeleton is flexible. This is because of the many joints, or junctures, where the bones meet. It is the flexibility of the many joints that permits you to move your body in the many ways that you do.

These movements are possible because of the way that the joints act. The simplest movement is that of a hinge joint. The opposing ends of two bones form a joint that permits movement in one plane, in one direction, up or down. The joints at the elbows, at the knees, and of the fingers and the toes are examples of hinge joints.

The bones of the wrists, the ankles, and the backbone make sliding joints with one another. Several faces of one of the bones are in contact with adjacent faces of other bones over which they can glide. Such joints permit movement in several directions.

The freest movement is that allowed by a ball-and-socket joint. You can imitate it by making a tight fist with one hand and surrounding it with the fingers of the other hand. See how you can turn and twist your fist! Your arms make such ball-and-socket joints with your shoulders; your legs make such joints with your hips.

A dislocation occurs when the bones of a joint are pushed out of alignment. Sometimes they snap back into place by themselves; if they do not, they have to be set. In such a dislocation, the ligaments of the joint will be sprained as the ends of the dislocated bones push the fibers beyond their ability to give. A ligament may even rupture completely. Such torn ligaments occur not uncommonly at the kneecap and at the shoulder.

Bones are made up of mineral matter, of which common table salt is an example; and of animal matter, of which the soft tissues of the body are examples. The mineral matter in bones makes them hard and rigid; the animal matter makes them somewhat flexible. The bones of young children have less mineral matter than do those of older girls and boys or of adults. Hence the bones of youngsters are less likely to break as they fall, tumble, and bounce about. With advancing age the bones become harder and more rigid as more mineral matter is added to them, causing them to break more readily.

When eager parents start young children walking at too early an age the youngsters may become bowlegged. Their leg bones are not yet hard and rigid enough to bear the weight of their bodies; consequently the leg bones bend or bow. This condition may result, also, from a lack of vitamin D in the diet or from a lack of sunlight on the bodies of young children. Vitamin D and sunlight help the body to add minerals to the bones.

There is a "soft bone" in the body that lacks the minerals necessary for rigidity. Bend and fold your ears to feel the flexible material that gives them their shape and keeps them erect. This is cartilage, or soft bone. It covers the surfaces of the bones where they form a joint, so that hard bone does not rub against hard bone. Disks of cartilage are found between the bones that make up the backbone; and rings of soft bone are found in the walls of the windpipe.

The bones of your skeleton also store minerals that you need for nutrition. The marrow that is found in many bones makes red blood cells.

The skeletal bones are organized into groups that have special functions. Thus the trunk includes the backbone, the hip girdle, the ribs, and the shoulder girdle; the head includes the bones of the skull. The bones that comprise the limbs are attached to the trunk at the shoulders and hips.

The backbone is made up of twenty-four separate bones that fit one on top of the other. There are seven in the neck, twelve in the chest region, and five in the small of the back. These bones are the vertebrae. The backbone is therefore also called the vertebral column. Disks of cartilage between the vertebrae keep the hard bone surfaces from rubbing against one another. The bones are held together firmly but flexibly by many ligaments and by the back muscles. These muscles are attached to the spines that extend from the sides and the back of each vertebra. Because of these spines, the name "spinal column," or just "spine," is often used for the backbone.

The structure of the backbone enables you to sit and to stand erect. Also, you can—under normal circumstances—bend, turn, twist, wriggle, and squirm without forcing the vertebrae out of alignment.

Each vertebra has a round opening in its center. To-gether, these openings form a canal down the spinal column, through which runs the spinal cord, a cable of nerves that originates in the brain. The spinal cord gives off branch nerves to the organs of the body and, in turn, receives nerves from these organs.

Many adults, even young ones, suffer from ailing backs. The cause may be a sprained ligament of the spine or a displacement of the bones where the spinal column makes a junction with the hip girdle. Or the cartilage disk between a pair of vertebrae may slip out of place and press on a nerve that enters or leaves the spinal cord—or on nerves that both enter *and* leave. This can cause severe pain in the neck, back, or legs, depending on the location of the slipped disk.

The disk may slip back into place if one rests in bed for some days or weeks. Sometimes, however, a doctor has to stretch the spine in an attempt to make the disk resume its normal position. Such stretching is called applying traction. If these methods fail, or if the disk becomes broken by its displacement, it may have to be removed by surgery.

You have probably read, or heard, of someone who suffered a broken neck after striking the bottom of a shallow pool when diving, or of someone whose back was broken after an automobile or airplane accident. Such injuries are broken vertebrae. The victim may become paralyzed and lose the use of his arms or legs—or both. This happens when the broken vertebrae have injured the nerves that control the movement of these organs.

The skull is set on the two top vertebrae of the spinal column. On one it can move from side to side; on the other it can move up and down. Between the two, the head has a considerable range of movement. The hard, box-like skull protects the sensitive, vital brain. The spinal cord, originating in the base of the brain, passes through an opening in the bottom of the skull into the canal that extends down the spinal column.

At the lower end of the vertebral column, the last vertebra is attached by ligaments to a large, thick, triangular bone—the sacrum, which, in turn, is attached to heavy bones on each side of it. Together they make up the pelvic girdle, which forms a foundation for the trunk skeleton. On the sides of the pelvic girdle are the sockets for the ball-and-socket joints by which the legs are attached to the trunk. At the lower end of the sacrum are four small bones—vertebrae that did not develop. These vertebrae make a sort of tail at the end of the backbone. These little bones are sometimes broken when one falls backward and lands hard on one's buttocks. The injury can be quite painful, and sometimes requires surgery.

Your chest gets its shape from twelve pairs of slender, curved, flat bones of different sizes. These are the ribs. One end of each rib is attached to a vertebra by a ligament. The front ends of the first seven pairs are attached by strong ligaments to the breastbone, or sternum, that you can feel in the front of your chest. The next three pairs are attached by ligaments to the ribs above them. The last two pairs—the lowest—are not attached in front; they are called the "floating ribs." Your ribs form a sort of basket that gives some protection to the heart and the lungs within the chest cavity.

At the top of the chest, in front, you can feel the collar bones, one on either side. In the back, at each side, you can feel the shoulder blades. These four bones comprise the shoulder girdle. At the sides, where they meet, the collar bones and the shoulder blades form sockets into which the upper arms fit, making ball-and-socket joints.

The bones of the upper and lower limbs are quite similar. As we have learned, the arms and the legs are both attached to the body by ball-and-socket joints. There are hinge joints both at the elbows and the knees, sliding joints in the wrists and the ankles, and hinge joints in the fingers and toes. Moreover, the arms and the legs are comparable in the relative size of the upper arms and legs, the lower arms and legs, the wrists and the ankles, the palms of the hands and the soles of the feet, and the fingers and toes.

There are differences, of course, between the arms and the legs, for they have quite different uses. Thus, the leg bones are much longer and stronger (except for the toes); the wrists have no bones comparable to the heel bones, which must bear the weight of the body and the pounding of locomotion. The forearms, however, have greater power to rotate at the elbows; and the longer fingers and thumbs of the hands enable you to grasp and handle things.

Besides serving as a framework for the body, the bones provide surfaces to which many muscles are attached. Together, these muscles and the skeleton give your body its shape and form. They enable you to sit and stand, bend and straighten up, walk and run, grasp and hold, push and pull, eat and talk, and make the many movements you do.

The muscles are made up of fibers that can shorten, or

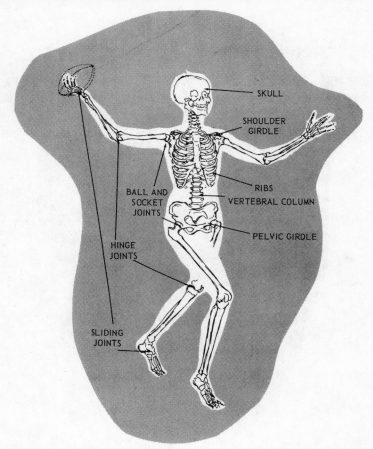

The flexibility of the skeleton results from the many joints made by its many bones

SKULL

SHOULDER
GIRDLE

RIBS

VERTEBRAL COLUMN

BALL AND
SOCKET
JOINTS

PELVIC GIRDLE

HINGE
JOINTS

SLIDING
JOINTS

contract, and thereby pull on the bones. The fibers, how-ever, cannot stretch. The action of the muscles is to con-tract and relax. They shorten and thicken to contract; they become longer and slimmer when they relax. They work in opposing pairs, with one muscle contracting as the other relaxes, and vice versa.

Muscles may be connected to cartilage, ligaments, and the skin as well as to bones, the connections being made

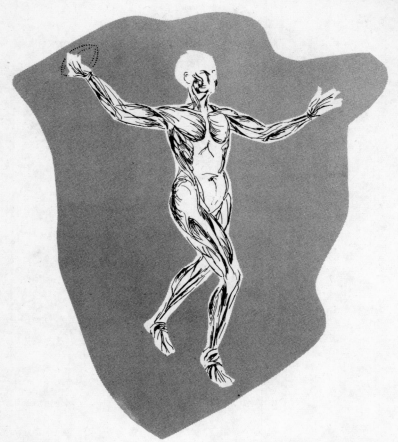

The skeletal muscles that are attached to the bones make possible their movement

by tendon fibers. These are the very tough, strong, and inelastic fibers that you can feel in some of the larger muscles. Feel the strong tendon that is attached to the back of the heel bone, then follow it until it enters the powerful calf muscle; or feel the large, tough tendons in back of the knee.

Muscles that are attached to the skeleton are called voluntary muscles. You can will them to work when you

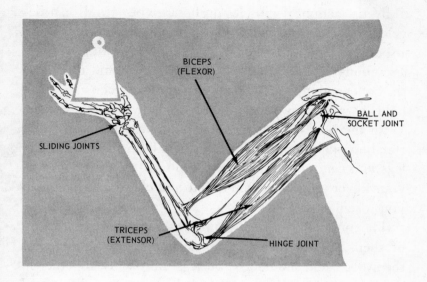

BICEPS
(FLEXOR)

BALL AND
SOCKET JOINT

SLIDING JOINTS

TRICEPS
(EXTENSOR)

HINGE JOINT

Action of opposing muscles

want them to. But there are some over which you have
lost control because you have not used them. For example,
you perhaps know some boy or girl who can wiggle one or
both of the ears a little. You, too, have the muscles for
doing so, but it would take a lot of practice to get them
active.

You can see and feel how muscles work as you raise and
lower your forearm. The biceps muscle is attached, at one
end, to the shoulder; at the other end, it is attached to the
inside of the forearm. When it shortens and thickens, it
pulls up the forearm. At the same time, the triceps muscle
on the back of the upper arm becomes longer and slimmer.
To lower the forearm, the triceps muscle shortens and
thickens as the biceps muscle becomes longer and slimmer.

By the action of muscles on bones, your hands can develop the numerous skills of which they are capable: using a spoon, a knife, a fork; writing and typewriting; sewing, assembling a radio kit—the list could go on and on. With the bones and muscles of your arm and hand you can grasp, hold, carry, throw, catch, push, pull, wave, and weave. With the bones and muscles of your legs you can walk, run, hop, skip, jump, kick, and dance. Using both arms and legs you can crawl, climb, and swim. Muscles attached to your lower jaw enable you to bite and chew, and they help you to talk and sing.

The muscles, too, are organized as a system so that many of them may cooperate. For example, many muscles of the arms, back, shoulders, and legs must work together in swimming, in serving a tennis ball—even in walking and standing erect. Muscles are strengthened by use; lack of use makes them soft and flabby. Exercise is necessary to keep your muscles in tone, in readiness to do the work that you expect of them.

All of the muscles of the body may be strengthened by suitable regular exercise; this is known as physical fitness. Exercise improves breathing, digestion, blood circulation, and the removal of waste from the body.

Girls and boys your age normally play so vigorously that exercise is no problem to you. But as you get older your play may become slower, and some of you may find yourselves watching others play rather than playing yourselves. You should form healthful exercise habits now and continue them into adult life. Such habits include walking briskly; swimming; jumping rope; rowing; playing tennis, table tennis, and handball. Exercises like these are general body conditioners.

There are, of course, many more good exercises which you can do at home. Your health education teacher has no doubt taught you some good setting-up exercises suitable for you. These may include bending over and touching your toes; lying in a prone position and raising your body from the waist without the help of your hands; doing push-ups from the floor while keeping your body straight; and jumping in place.

Many adults believe they are following a program of exercise if they play golf once a week or bowl or ski. The soreness and stiffness that many of them feel after doing so is proof that such activity is no substitute for regular exercise. Their activity is recreational rather than body-conditioning.

The bones and muscles of your back, chest, and shoulders are responsible for your posture in sitting and standing. Good posture not only improves your appearance, but is necessary for proper breathing since it allows the chest to expand more fully. It also allows the internal organs to lie in their proper positions and therefore to function better.

You can train your muscles to support your bones in a good postural position. Sit well back in a chair, supporting your trunk on the end of your spinal column, and rest your feet squarely on the floor in front of you. (Slouching puts the support on the wrong bones and muscles.) In standing, the feet should be parallel, the back straight, the shoulders square, and the chin up.

If you develop good posture now you will not have to

take corrective exercises later to overcome a posture defect such as round shoulders, arched or sway back, hollow chest, side curvature of the spine, or flat feet. The proper functioning of the skeletal and muscular systems is essential for good posture and good health.

The skeletal and muscular systems are two of the eight system organizations that make up the total organization of your body. You will learn about the others as you read the chapters that follow.

:two:

Selecting your food supply

If you had the job of choosing the family's food for a week, how would you go about it? You would want to include your favorite foods, of course, but would you be bewildered by the great variety of foods in the supermarket?

It would help if you knew more about your body's needs for food. The inches and pounds that you keep adding to your stature come from the food that you eat. Food is essential, too, in repairing bodily injuries. And all your work and play require the energy that is stored in fuels found in your food.

One may eat enough food to satisfy the body's requirements for growth and energy, and still feel and act below par, with little vigor. One may even suffer from some illness because of a deficiency in the food intake. The body,

A supermarket

then, must also have the proper food for protection against certain diseases.

Selecting foods from the thousands of items in a supermarket becomes somewhat simpler when you know just what there is in them that your body actually needs and uses for optimum efficiency.

Food chemists find only six different substances in all of the various foods that the body needs and utilizes to maintain health. These are the food nutrients. Proteins, minerals, and water are nutrients that are used for growth and the repair of cells. Fats and carbohydrates (sugar and starch) are fuels that supply energy. Proteins are sometimes used for fuel as well. Vitamins are protective nutrients.

The selection of foods is made easier when they are grouped according to their nutrient contents and the sources from which they come. We shall make four groupings. You will find the foods in a supermarket grouped similarly. For a healthful diet you should eat some foods from each of the four groups every day.

The meat, fish, and poultry group (eggs included) consists of foods of animal origin, rich in proteins. In meats, most people prefer the muscular parts—steaks, roasts, and chops, for example. However, the variety meats—liver, kidneys, sweetbreads, and the like—are especially rich in minerals and vitamins, though they are not generally as popular as the muscular parts.

Items in the milk and milk products group also come from animals. Milk, the mainstay of infants, supplies almost all of the necessary nutrients and is important in your diet as a food supplement. Cream, butter, and creamy cheeses are made from milk fat, and are good energy, or fuel, foods. Milk fat is also a good source of vitamin A, and whole milk and cheeses made from it supply proteins as well. Milk also is rich in calcium, the mineral that makes strong bones and teeth.

The cereal group is, of course, of plant origin. Here you find the well-known grains—wheat, rice, corn, rye, oats, and barley. Bread made from wheat, rye, or corn flour is called the "staff of life" because it is the basic food of many people throughout the world. Rolls, muffins, biscuits, cakes, cookies, and pies are grain products, too, as are the raw and cooked breakfast cereal foods.

Cereals have a high starch content and are principal fuel foods. They are also valuable for their protein, mineral, and vitamin contents, if they are eaten as *whole* grains. Because many people prefer the appearance or taste of white bread, wheat is refined in milling. This process removes from the grain the husk in which the minerals and vitamins are found, as well as the germ in which the protein is found. White rice is similarly produced from the whole grain by removing the husk.

The bread baked from refined flour may appear pure in color, but it is poor in nutrients. Bakers now enrich white bread by adding some of the minerals and vitamins, even protein, that were removed in the milling. Look at the wrapper of a loaf of white bread to see how it has been enriched.

The vegetable and fruit group is also of plant origin. The green leafy vegetables (the varieties of lettuce and of cabbage, spinach, turnip and beet tops) are especially rich sources of minerals and vitamins. The root vegetables (potatoes, yams, carrots, turnips, and beets) are high in

The four food groups

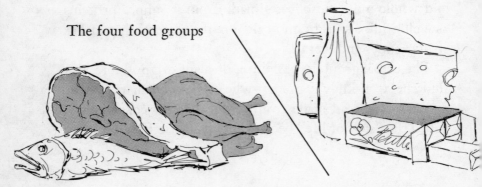

starch; and the yellow ones are valuable for their vitamin content. Fruits have a high sugar content and are valuable for minerals and vitamins. The citrus fruits—oranges, grapefruits, and lemons—are especially rich in vitamin C.

Oils pressed from olives, peanuts, coconuts, soybeans, and from corn grains are abundant sources of fuel for the body. Doctors believe that vegetable fats are more healthful than animal fats, which are thought to injure the blood vessels as one grows older. For this reason, many people use oleomargarine instead of butter. Made from vegetable oils, oleomargarine is enriched with vitamin A and colored to resemble butter.

Mineral salts, of which table salt is a familiar example, are found in foods in all groups. Altogether, your body needs only about one ounce of these salts a day, and half of this need is for table salt, as it occurs naturally in foods. The mineral salts supply the body with calcium, iron, sodium, potassium, phosphorous, iodine, fluorine, and magnesium. They are used in the body to make bones and teeth; to make red blood; to make chemicals that are needed for the work of the organs; and to enable the muscles to work properly.

Sometimes you may need to increase your intake of a

particular salt. It can be obtained from a food especially rich in it, such as milk for calcium, and liver for iron to build red blood. Sea foods, especially shellfish, are rich in iodine; the body needs iodine to make a certain chemical that helps in energy production. Seasoning food with iodized salt—ordinary table salt supplemented by iodine— also helps to increase one's supply of this important mineral.

Mineral salts may be added to drinking water as well as to food. Iodine is added to water in regions where it is missing in natural water and in the soil. The salt of fluorine, which has been found to reduce tooth decay in children, is also being added to the drinking water of many communities.

When needed by a patient's body, particular minerals may be prescribed as medicines by a doctor.

All the vitamins that you need for an entire two-month period would not fill a teaspoon. Isn't it remarkable that so small a quantity of nutrients should have so important a role in the healthful functioning of your body?

When vitamins were discovered, a little more than fifty years ago, they were given letter names: A, B, C, D. This was because their chemical nature, or composition, was not known. Since then chemists not only have analyzed their composition, but also are able to manufacture some of them in laboratories.

On the wrappers and labels of most packaged foods you will see the names of the vitamins contained in them. If you also know the natural food sources of the vitamins, you can make diet choices that will include all the ones necessary for healthful living.

You should know the six most common vitamins listed here, and be sure to include them in your food intake. If you do, you will very likely get the others that you need.

Name of vitamin	*Food sources*	*Uses in the body*
Vitamin A	Milk, butter, egg yolks, liver, kidneys, green and yellow vegetables, tomatoes	Helps to keep the skin soft and smooth; helps to keep the eyelids moist and free of infection; helps one to see in dim light.
Thiamin (B1)	Whole grains, peas, beans, pork, nuts, yeast, green vegetables	Helps to produce energy; helps keep nerve tissue healthy; promotes good appetite and digestion.
Riboflavin (B2)	Whole grains, milk, eggs, nuts, liver, green vegetables	Helps to produce energy; helps to prevent sores on face, lips, and tongue.
Niacin (part of B group)	Whole grains, meat, fish, liver, peanuts, green vegetables	Helps to keep the skin, nerves, and digestive organs healthy.
Ascorbic acid (C)	Citrus fruits—oranges, grapefruits, lemons, tomatoes	Helps in forming healthy bones and teeth; helps to keep the tiny blood tubes in good condition; helps to prevent bleeding in gums and skin.
Calciferol (D)	Milk and dairy products, cod liver and other fish liver oils; the skin makes it in sunlight	Needed for normal growth of bones and teeth; regulates use of calcium and phosphorus in the body.

A severe lack of vitamins in a person's diet can result in a vitamin-deficiency disease. For example, night blindness and a disease characterized by dry, scaly eyelids may be caused by a lack of vitamin A.

Beriberi, scurvy, and rickets are other vitamin-deficiency diseases. These illnesses are common when people do not have an abundance and a wide selection of foods, and when poverty prevails.

Many people suffer not from a lack, but from a shortage of one or another vitamin. Symptoms of this may be lack of pep, a poor appetite, irritability, or difficulty (caused by night blindness) in finding a seat in a darkened theatre. You are not likely to suffer from such a shortage if you choose vitamin-rich foods and do not waste the vitamins.

A vitamin and mineral loss occurs, as we learned, when flour and rice are refined. Blanched celery and the pale green or white inner leaves of lettuce and cabbage may have a cleaner look, but most of their minerals and vitamins are in the green stalks and in the green outer leaves that too often are thrown into the garbage pail. When fruits and vegetables are peeled before eating, their mineral and vitamin content is thrown away.

Vitamins are also lost in food handling. Fruit is generally picked before it is ripe because it is better shipped that way. But tree-ripened fruit has a higher vitamin content than does fruit ripened in storage. Green leafy vegetables that are allowed to wilt and dry lose most of their thiamin and ascorbic acid.

A great loss of vitamins takes place in the cooking of food. Vitamin A is destroyed if the foods are heated in open pots. If the liquid in which vegetables are cooked is not used to make a soup or gravy, thiamin and ascorbic acid are poured down the drain.

Most foods have a considerable water content. Dry breakfast cereals have the least, while leafy vegetables, tomatoes, and milk are more than 90 percent water. Since you lose about nine pints of water a day, you must replace this loss with water from food and beverages or you run the risk of becoming dehydrated—the dried-out state that occurs when your water output is greater than your intake. Cells in your throat act as your thirst-control, reminding you to take water.

Now that you know what you should eat, you should know how much to eat. You have a built-in gauge, your appetite. Hunger is the body's call for food. If you eat when you are hungry and stop when your hunger is satisfied—or a little before—you will usually get enough food for your body's needs. You probably eat a little more or less at different times, depending on how active you have been. This is healthful eating, "eating to live."

But there are those who "live to eat." Some boys and girls eat so much at mealtimes that they can hardly move, and then indulge in between-meals snacks of candy, cookies, peanuts, and ice cream. If carried into adult life, such eating habits may become a health hazard.

How much food your body needs, and how much is supplied by each portion of food that you eat, can be exactly measured in calories. These are units of heat energy, just as ounces are units of weight. Where ounces measure the weight of food, calories measure its fuel value.

Even while you rest or sleep, work goes on in your body. You breathe, your heart beats, and your brain remains active. All your cells carry on some activity. Besides, the internal temperature of the body must be maintained. The condition within your body while you're asleep may be compared to that of a banked fire. The necessary fuel for these activities comes from the stored food in your body.

Numerous experiments have been performed to determine how many calories of food are needed for these minimal activities. For boys and girls of your age group, it would be about eighteen calories per day for boys and fourteen for girls for each pound of body weight. Thus, a hundred-pounder would require from eighteen hundred to fourteen hundred calories of food per day for minimal need, according to sex.

From other experiments, we know how much food, measured in calories, is needed for almost any activity in your day. Here are a few examples. An eighty-pound girl or boy uses twelve calories in dressing and undressing (allowing fifteen minutes for each). Sixteen calories are used in sitting for an hour watching television or reading a book, and fifty-six in practicing the piano diligently for an hour. Seventy calories are needed if you dance for half an hour (less for a slow waltz, more for a fast dance). One hundred and thirty-two are required if you run around for half an hour in a fast game.

The total food needs for a day of normal activity, measured in calories, comes to between thirteen and eighteen hundred. This must be added to the calories for minimal need. Thus, on the average, a boy weighing one hundred pounds requires a total of thirty-one hundred to thirty-six hundred calories of food a day, and a girl of the same age and weight will need about one-fifth less. Some girls and boys require more or less than the average, depending on their activities.

Lists are available giving the number of calories in an average serving of most foods, and many packaged foods have such information on the carton or wrapper. If you care to, you can figure your calorie intake and compare it with your calorie need. You need not make every meal a lesson in arithmetic, for eating should be enjoyed; but you *may* have to count calories if you develop a diet problem.

Your diet—the combination of foods that you eat—is a healthful one if your growth rate is normal; if you have plenty of energy and pep for work and play; and if you are free from any vitamin-deficiency diseases.

Your diet has undoubtedly been planned for you by your mother, but if you had to make the food selection yourself, do you know how you would go about it? You would, of course, remember to select foods from all four food groups to insure a mixed diet with all nutrients included.

You do not need equal parts of all nutrients in your diet. Your body thrives if your diet includes 10 to 15 percent of proteins; 25 to 30 percent of fats; 60 to 70 percent of carbohydrates. Such a diet is a balanced one.

Being overweight is generally, but not always, a diet problem. It is nearly always a personal problem. Overweight boys and girls are sometimes teased, and are often embarrassed by their appearances. Even in their pre-teen years they may not feel their best and play their hardest; and unless they lose weight, they will be storing up future health problems for themselves.

Overweight youngsters may start their reducing diets by simply eating less at each meal, especially less of foods with a high calorie count such as bread, cakes, cookies, potatoes, and butter. Then they should cut out the in-between snacks. This will not be hard and will reduce the calorie intake by about five hundred, which is a safe reduction. If this does not do the job, a special diet should be prescribed and directed by a doctor.

Though some boys and girls appear underweight, it may be simply a matter of body form. Some youngsters are naturally tall and slender. If one is only a little under-weight for one's height and age, increasing the food intake should remedy the situation. It need not be of protein foods especially, because most people in this country have an adequate protein intake. However, a boy or girl who is considerably underweight and lacking in vigor should seek medical advice.

Expensive foods are not necessarily the most nutritious. The proteins in chuck meat are the same as those in a porterhouse steak that costs much more. Meats and fish are expensive protein foods, but plant foods such as whole grains, peas, beans, and lentils have a good protein content and are also inexpensive.

Many people have strong beliefs or preferences that limit their food choices. Vegetarians do not eat foods of animal origin, for example. A so-called dairy diet is a vegetarian diet with milk, cheese, and eggs added. Some people will eat only "natural" foods, meaning foods that have not undergone any manufacturing. They will eat honey rather than white sugar, for example.

In some African countries, tribesmen will not drink an animal's milk, believing it to be animal waste, but they will drink the animal's blood. In India, where cows are held to be sacred, they may be fed by people close to starvation, but these people will not use the cows as food. Some people will not eat certain animals or certain parts of animals, certain fish, or certain shellfish.

Like most boys and girls, you no doubt have your likes and dislikes, and you are probably slow to experiment with untried foods. But with time, and with patience on the part of your parents, you will gradually add to your food likes so that your diet will be greatly extended and enriched. Then you can choose what you like and still choose a diet for healthful living, a diet that will be greatly varied because of your varied tastes.

:three:
Your food goes through a mill

How would you like your chicken for dinner—boiled, broiled, grilled, barbecued, baked, roasted, fried, or creamed? It is an important question because the appearance, odor, taste—even the thought of foods you enjoy—helps ready the organs of your digestive system for their work.

Your mouth may water when you see, smell, or think of food. Saliva will begin to flow, ready to do its part in digesting the food you will eat.

Soon after you have taken a bite of food, it no longer resembles what it formerly was. Your teeth will have cut, crushed, and ground it into bits. Then, mixed with saliva, the food will become a doughy mass, and will start through your food mill.

All the food you eat is first broken up, then changed

into simple substances that your cells can use for building material, for fuel, and for making chemicals needed for the work of the body.

Changing food into substances that your cells can use is called digestion, and is the work of the organs of the digestive system. This system includes a long muscular tube (the alimentary canal), and a number of digestive glands, chemical factories, some of which are in the canal, and some outside but feeding into it.

Infants, at first, have a liquid diet—either mothers' milk or a liquid formula—since they have no teeth. The first tooth appears at about the age of six months. In the meantime, some mashed foods will have been added to the baby's diet. At about twenty-four months, the child has twenty teeth—his first complete set—known as the primary (or temporary) teeth. The parents now teach the child to chew solid food well (although he has already had solid mashed food); this is a healthful eating habit to form at an early age. The youngster will also get his first lessons in the care of his teeth.

Tooth decay is caused by bacteria. When bits of food— especially sweets—are left in the spaces between the teeth, they are eaten by bacteria that exist in the mouth. These bacteria produce acids that destroy the hard enamel covering of the teeth and cause them to decay. Proper brushing, at regular intervals, removes most of the food particles and helps to prevent decay. The toothbrush should have stiff bristles, but not so stiff and hard that they will make the gums bleed.

Do you use a proper brush and brush your teeth correctly? You should brush down on the upper teeth, including the gums, front and back. Similarly, brush up on the lower teeth. Use a scrubbing motion across the tops of the molar teeth in the back. In this way the bristles can get more readily into the spaces between the teeth to remove the food particles.

The teeth should be brushed after every meal, but if you are away from home and unable to do this, then you should at least rinse your mouth thoroughly with water. This will remove many of the food particles, and you can complete the job when you get home.

A dentist should be visited regularly. He will keep the temporary teeth in good repair, and will remove any that do not come out when they should. Such care is necessary to insure that the permanent teeth come through in their correct positions, with the upper and lower teeth properly aligned. As a result, the permanent teeth will look better and will work better.

You have lost your primary teeth, and now have your permanent set, which is complete except for your third molars—the wisdom teeth—which you will get when you are about eighteen.

Your upper and lower set of permanent teeth each includes four cutting and two cutting-biting teeth, used to cut off bite-size pieces of food; and eight (later ten) crushing and grinding teeth. This is the last set that nature will provide for you. If your diet includes the minerals necessary to make your permanent teeth hard and strong, and if you care for them properly, they should last you a lifetime, barring accidents. Should you neglect them, your next teeth will be supplied by a dentist and will, of course, be false.

Perhaps you, like many boys and girls of your age, wear braces to change the position of some of your teeth. Braces improve the bite—the alignment of the upper and lower teeth—so that you can chew your food better, and they may also improve the appearance of your teeth. This kind of dental correction is called orthodontia.

You will want to take good care of your teeth, because they are necessary for good digestion. The more thoroughly the food is chewed, the more readily and completely it will be changed as it moves through the digestive system. In the process of chewing, the food is mixed with saliva containing digestive enzymes.

Enzymes are chemicals produced in certain glands in tissues of the body. There are many different kinds serving many different functions. They are able to bring about changes in substances without themselves being changed or destroyed in the process. Life would not be possible without the work of enzymes. Digestive enzymes, which are in the secretions from digestive glands, change the nature of nutrients in food.

Such changes begin in the mouth, as we stated earlier. Around the lower jaw and at the sides of the upper jaw there are three pairs of digestive glands—the salivary glands. They produce the saliva that enters the mouth through tubes or ducts. The digestive enzyme in saliva can change starch into a simple kind of sugar—like that found in grapes.

This explains why a plain cracker or piece of bread, if

kept in the mouth and chewed long enough, tastes sweet after a while. The more thoroughly you chew your food, and the more thoroughly it is mixed with saliva, the more starch is changed into sugar in the mouth. Another enzyme in saliva begins to change fats.

From the mouth, the food is pushed into the throat by the tongue. There are a number of openings in the back of the throat: one pair leads into the nostrils; one opening leads into the windpipe; another leads into the food pipe called the gullet, or esophagus.

As the muscles of the throat contract to push the food mass along, a muscular flap closes over the first and the second openings (those leading to nostrils and windpipe) so that the food is directed into the third—the gullet. This is how you perform the simple act of swallowing.

Sometimes, if you try to talk as you eat, the flap covering the nostrils and windpipe is caught open, and the food goes into the wrong opening. You sputter or cough, or both, until the food is dislodged. This can be quite uncomfortable, and in the windpipe it can be dangerous, for the food may shut off the supply of air to the lungs.

The gullet is a muscular tube about nine to ten inches long. The food mass does not drop down the gullet, as it might through a chute, but is pushed along. A circular muscle in the wall of the gullet contracts behind the mass, while the muscles in front of it relax. A succession of such muscular movements pushes the food along until it enters the stomach. This explains why an astronaut can swallow food while he and the food are weightless in outer space, and why you *can* swallow food while upside down in a headstand or handstand.

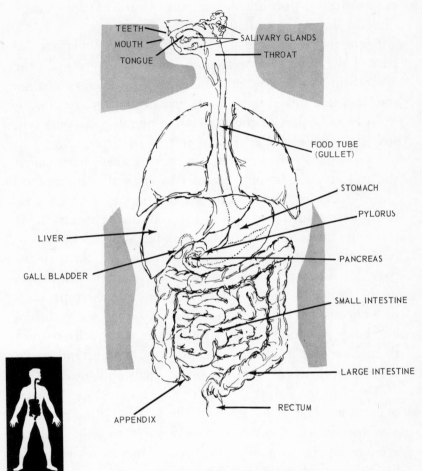

TEETH
MOUTH
TONGUE
SALIVARY GLANDS
THROAT
FOOD TUBE (GULLET)
STOMACH
PYLORUS
LIVER
PANCREAS
GALL BLADDER
SMALL INTESTINE
LARGE INTESTINE
RECTUM
APPENDIX

Organs of the digestive system

The muscles of the alimentary canal, of which the gullet is a small part, are not voluntary; they are not part of the voluntary skeletal muscular system. In other words, you cannot will them to work. Since the muscles do the work automatically, you are not usually aware of the passage of food down the gullet.

From the gullet, the food passes into the wide, saclike part of the stomach, the fundus, where it may remain for several hours. The enzyme in saliva continues to change the food it is mixed with into sugar even after the food is in this saclike part of the stomach. The saliva enzyme will stop its work in the narrower end of the stomach.

When the food passes on into this narrower part, called the pylorus, the strong muscles in its wall squeeze and churn it, causing the food to mix thoroughly with the gastric juices, made by glands in the wall of the stomach. At this stage the food resembles a thick pea soup.

Another enzyme now begins to change the protein particles. This enzyme is produced in the single-cell glands in the lining of the stomach. Digestion changes proteins into chemicals called amino acids. There are many different kinds of amino acids. From them your cells rebuild themselves, repair themselves, make new cells, and make the many chemicals that the body needs and uses.

A muscular valve at the end of the stomach opens every once in a while to let some of the souplike food mixture pass into the small intestine. This is a narrow tube with an average length of about twenty-two feet in an adult. It lies coiled within your abdomen.

As the food is squeezed and pushed along in the small intestine, the liquid is mixed with different digestive juices. One such juice comes directly into the intestine from millions of cell glands in its wall; another comes through a duct from the pancreas, a gland that lies behind the stomach; a third comes from the liver, also through a duct.

Digestion is completed in the small intestine by the enzymes in these juices. All carbohydrates are changed into simple sugars; all proteins are changed into amino acids; and all fats are changed into fatty acids.

These sugars, amino acids, and fatty acids are needed by cells in all parts of the body. The blood stream carries the digested foods away from the tubular intestine and distributes them to the various cells throughout the body. But how do these materials get into the blood?

If you were to look at a piece of carpet with a magnifying glass, you would see that it is made up of countless erect threads. That is what gives carpets their "plushy" feel. When the lining of the small intestine is examined with a microscope, its wall is similarly found to have countless microscopic projecting threads. These are the villi. A single layer of extremely thin, flat cells covers each villus. And within each one there are even more minute blood tubes.

As the muscles squeeze the contents of the small intestine, the digested nutrients are brought into close contact with the villi. The sugar, the amino acids, and the fatty acids are able to pass through the covering cells and into the tiny blood tubes, although neither is porous. This is called absorption.

The blood from the small intestine flows to all parts of the body, carrying food for all the cells. They absorb the materials they need as the blood streams by. We may say, then, that the purpose of digestion is to make the food we eat absorbable.

Blood containing the absorbed nutrients passes through the liver on the way to the heart. The liver changes some of the sugar in the blood into an animal starch, and stores it until the body's cells need fuel. Then the starch is changed back into sugar and enters the blood stream once more.

Many people eat far more protein than they need for growth and repair. It is not healthful to have an excess of amino acids, the products of protein digestion, in the cell environment. In the liver some of the excess amino acids are changed into sugar, and then into animal starch, and are stored there. More of the excess amino acids are changed into urea, a waste product that is removed from the blood, and then from the body by the kidneys.

But what happens to those foods we eat that are indigestible? Many plant foods contain a great deal of such indigestible material. Enzymes cannot digest the walls of plant cells, for example. Those found in the skins of fruits and vegetables, the fibers of leafy vegetables, the husks of grains, and the coats of seeds are especially thick. Such foods must be thoroughly chewed in the mouth and mashed in the stomach if the useful nutrients within the cells are to be absorbed by the body.

The indigestible material is useful, however. Such bulky roughage gives the muscles of the alimentary canal something to work on. Their contractions must be extremely strong to break up the food, to mix it with the digestive juices, to move it along the canal, and to bring the digested food in contact with the villi. If all your food were predigested—taken in capsules—it would not be healthful. The muscles of the alimentary canal would lose their tone, become sluggish, and perhaps cease to function.

The indigestible material in food is eventually pushed

into the large intestine. Although it is only about five feet long, it is called large because its diameter is greater than that of the small intestine. The large intestine makes a loop around the small intestine.

Extending from the large intestine, close to its junction with the small one, is a wormlike tube averaging three and a half inches in length. This is the appendix, an organ that does not appear to have any use in the body. If it becomes infected it can be removed by surgery without impairing digestion or any other body function.

As the undigested or indigestible food passes along through the large intestine, much of the water in the mixture is absorbed from it through the intestinal wall. To the waste there is added slimy mucus from cells in the wall; bacteria that live in the large intestine; and bile that comes from the liver. This mixture gathers at the lower end of the large intestine, the rectum, where it may remain for a day or more. Finally, the pressure of the mass causes the muscular valve at the end of the alimentary canal to open. When the muscles in the wall of the rectum contract and force out the waste mass (called feces), this is known as a bowel movement. (Bowel is a common name for the large intestine.)

While it is not necessary, it is a good lifetime health habit to void these wastes at a regular time each day to avoid constipation, the clogging of the large intestine. Bacteria feed upon the clogged matter and produce poisonous substances that are absorbed by the blood and carried about the body.

People who fail to form the habit of regularity may become dependent upon mild laxatives that stimulate the muscles of the large intestine, or strong purgatives that draw water from the blood to help clear clogged material from the rectum.

It will help in developing regular habits if your diet includes plenty of bulky roughage foods such as leafy vegetables and whole-grain cereals; plenty of water, both in foods and as beverages; and some foods that are naturally mildly laxative such as oranges and prunes. Regular exercise, sufficient rest and recreation, plenty of fresh air, and freedom from worry will also help promote regularity.

One may have frequent and watery bowel movements. This condition is called diarrhea. It results when the wall of the large intestine has been irritated—by something in the food that has been eaten, by an infection in the organ, or by a medicine. The contraction of the muscles that make up the wall of the large intestine are speeded up. Consequently, too little water is absorbed from the wastes in the bowel. Diarrhea is often accompanied by cramping pains. The movements generally stop in a day or so. If diarrhea persists, the advice of a doctor may be required.

Have you ever had an upset stomach? Then you know what indigestion is. Common causes are: eating your food too hurriedly and in large chunks; overeating; rushing off to play immediately after eating; and eating unripe fruit.

The stomach muscles have to work harder than usual if your teeth have not done their job; and they have even more trouble if you have eaten too much. Exercise too soon after eating draws blood from the digestive glands, where the digestive enzymes are made, to the arms and legs, so that the supply of digestive enzymes is reduced. The enzymes cannot get at the nutrients in the hard cells of unripe fruit, and again indigestion occurs. The stomach and small intestine respond with cramps and pain—punishment for ignoring good eating habits.

An unhappy mental state—sadness, anger, fear—can affect your digestive glands and cause indigestion. Have you ever had your mouth become dry because of fright or anger? The salivary glands seem to "dry up," and that is exactly what happens: They stop making juice. Mealtime, then, should be a pleasant, relaxed time; if you come to the table fretful or troubled, you may not digest your food even if you succeed in swallowing it.

Under normal conditions, it takes about ten hours for your meal to be digested and absorbed. After you have eaten, provided you are physically and mentally well, you will not be aware of the complex work that is being performed by your digestive system as it converts the food into materials your cells can use.

Hunger pangs are your signals and reminders that your body can use more food. The interval between meals depends, to a large extent, on how you have become conditioned to eating—on the mealtimes to which you have become accustomed. It will depend, too, on the kinds and quantity of food that you eat at each meal. If you wait until you are hungry before you eat you will not burden your digestive system. The previous meal will be well along toward complete digestion and absorption. You will be eating healthfully with respect to digestion.

:four:

Energy for your work and play

After a fast, exciting game of Ping-Pong, tennis, or hand-ball you feel warm and wet; you breathe hard and fast; your heart pounds. This is what happens when you work hard. Even play is work—of a happy kind.

Work requires energy, and this is stored in fuels. A steam engine uses wood, coal, oil, or even gas as its source of energy; an automobile uses gasoline; you use food, especially fats and carbohydrates. All these fuels obtain their energy in the first place from the same source, the sun.

Green plant cells are able to use light energy from the sun to combine carbon dioxide (a gas that is plentiful in the air) with water to make sugar. Plant cells are able to change this into starch or fat or, with the addition of certain minerals, into proteins. Animals eat the plant nutrients and change them into animal nutrients. We eat both plant and animal foods, and thus get our fuel from both. Our food could be called "canned" sunlight.

Until scientists discovered how to release the immense store of atomic energy, machines (except those operated by electric batteries) got their power by burning fuel. Fuel burns as long as oxygen is supplied to it, producing intense heat and flame and giving off carbon dioxide and water.

Though the fuel in your body does not burn, you use oxygen in energy production, and you give off carbon dioxide and water. You also produce heat, although not of great intensity. This is the function of respiration—to produce energy for use by the body.

As you know, you replenish your supply of fuel several times a day, at mealtimes preferably. And you store a considerable amount of fuel as body fat, and as animal starch in the liver and the muscles.

You get oxygen by breathing air, one fifth of which is oxygen. But you must replenish your supply of oxygen frequently, eighteen to twenty times a minute. This is your breathing rate. It increases greatly when you work or play hard.

Air normally enters the body through the nostrils, except in swimming when it is necessary to breathe through the mouth. In passing through the nasal passages, the air is cleaned and warmed. Dust and germs are caught by small hairs, and by the sticky mucus that is produced by cells of the membranes lining the nasal passages. From time to time, you get rid of the dried or moist mucus, along with the germs and dust, by blowing your nose.

Beneath the thin lining membrane of the nasal passages, there are many tiny blood vessels through which warm blood flows. The air is warmed as it passes over them.

The nasal passages of some children become so clogged that they breathe through them with difficulty and become mouth breathers. These children do not have the protection that breathing through the nostrils provides. Adenoids —growths in back of the nasal passages—are frequently the cause of clogging. They may be removed easily by a doctor.

Air that is entering the body passes through the nostrils into the throat. Here are the openings into the food tube (the gullet), which is *closed* except when food is being swallowed; and into the air tube (the windpipe), which in *open* except when food is being swallowed.

In the throat there are also two small openings, one on either side, leading into tiny tubes (the Eustachian tubes) that are connected to the middle ears. Through these tubes, air from the throat is passed into the middle ears; without air, the eardrums could not function, and you would not be able to hear.

Germs from a sore throat may be forced into the ears through these tubes, causing infections, if the nose is not blown properly. Both nostrils should be kept open, and the nose should always be blown gently. Often a person will close one nostril in order to force the mucus out of the nostril being blown. Provided he blows gently and provided the nostril being blown is not completely plugged, or "stopped up," this is usually safe. However, if the nostril being blown *is* completely plugged, and he

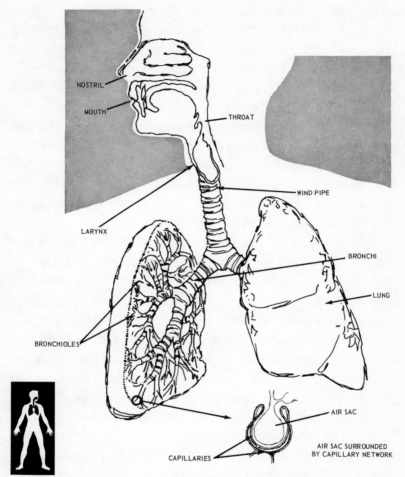

NOSTRIL

MOUTH

THROAT

WIND PIPE

LARYNX

BRONCHI

LUNG

BRONCHIOLES

AIR SAC

AIR SAC SURROUNDED
BY CAPILLARY NETWORK

CAPILLARIES

Organs of the respiratory system

closes the other and blows, he will feel a pressure in his ears, and there is a chance that he may have forced germs into the middle ear.

Air that has gone from the nose into the throat next

enters the windpipe. At the top of the windpipe is a box-like part made of cartilage that can be felt in the front of the neck. This is the larynx, or voice box; in people with thin necks, you can see it bob up and down as they gulp or swallow. The larynx is pointed in front, and the point is called the Adam's apple.

Within the voice box are the vocal cords—flaps of tissue that vibrate as air is forced out over them. The vibrations produce sounds that are changed into speech in the mouth and throat. The voice becomes husky (hoarse) when the vocal cords are swollen from such abuse as shouting or yelling, or when the cords are infected.

Below the larynx is the trachea, a flexible tube about four inches long and about one inch thick. Rings of cartilage in its wall keep the trachea open. The cells that line it have very tiny hairlike threads which, by their movement, push out dust and germs that come into the trachea. An occasional cough gets rid of the irritants.

The trachea divides to form two main branches, the bronchi, on each side of the chest. As the bronchi enter the lungs they, in turn, divide to form many smaller branches, the bronchioles. The trachea branches out much as a tree does. First, there is the trunk (the trachea), then two main branches (the bronchi) which divide into count-less smaller branches (the bronchioles). The larger bron-chioles have cartilage rings in their walls. The smallest ones end in microscopic bags, or air sacs.

The lungs are not like hollow bags, but are made up of millions of these air sacs, which give the lungs their spongy texture. The two lungs fill the chest cavity except for the space occupied by the heart, some large blood vessels, and the gullet. The capacity of the lungs—the amount of air they can hold—depends on the size of a person's chest, and that, in turn, depends on the person's body development and age.

There are, then, four organs of the respiratory system: the nose; the throat; the windpipe, which includes the larynx, the trachea, and the bronchi. The fourth is the pair of lungs, with their millions of bronchioles and tiny air sacs.

Air, however, does not flow into and out of these organs. This is accomplished by the cooperative action of the breathing muscles. The breathing muscles are: those that are attached directly to the ribs; and the diaphragm, an umbrella-shaped, muscular partition that separates the cavity of the chest from that of the abdomen.

As you have already read, the ribs are attached in front to the breastbone by strong ligaments; and in the back, to vertebrae by sliding joints. When the rib muscles contract, the basket of ribs is raised and the chest is enlarged in diameter. You can feel this happening if you place your hands on the sides of your chest. At the same time, the diaphragm contracts and becomes flatter. This increases the depth of the chest from top to bottom. Thus, when the chest expands it increases in diameter and in depth.

The lungs are elastic, so that when the chest expands they stretch and fill the enlarged space. The air in the lungs naturally expands, so that air pressure is reduced. Now the pressure of the air *outside* the body, at the nostrils, is greater than the pressure of the air in the lungs. As a consequence, air flows into the lungs.

Once the air has filled the lungs, the contracted rib muscles and the diaphragm relax, returning to their original positions. The chest becomes smaller; the lungs are compressed; the pressure of the air inside them is increased until it is greater than the pressure on the *outside*. Now air is pushed out of the lungs; you exhale when it is pushed out of them.

While sitting quietly reading this book, you are inhaling between half a pint and a pint of air. During active play this amount will be doubled or tripled, and you will breathe much more often and much more deeply. With your chest expanded to its utmost and the lungs fully inflated, the lungs have a capacity of about six pints of air. This capacity is somewhat greater for boys than for girls. The lungs cannot be completely deflated, or emptied. Some air always remains trapped in the air sacs.

When you are inactive for a time, the air in the lungs becomes "stale," and contains a larger percentage of carbon dioxide. This is especially so in the upper regions of the lungs, which expand and contract less than the lower regions do. This difference exists because of the difference in the structure of the ribs in the two regions. The first few pairs of ribs are shorter, and they are not raised as much as the longer ribs of the lower region. You can feel with your hands how much more the lower part of the chest expands than the upper part. Deep breathing exchanges a greater volume of air, including that from the upper part of the lungs.

Since the breathing muscles are voluntary, you can control them to a certain extent with your will. You can, if you keep your mind on it, regulate the rate and depth of breathing. You can even deliberately stop breathing for a short while by holding your breath. You do this when you swim under water without an aqualung. Some people, with practice, are able to hold their breaths for as long as a minute or two.

You have an automatic control center, called the respiratory center, that regulates your breathing under normal conditions. This center is a cluster of nerve cells that are very sensitive to carbon dioxide, located in a part of the brain called the medulla. When the blood flows through this cluster, the carbon dioxide in the blood causes the cells to send nerve impulses (command signals) to the breathing muscles; the muscles immediately contract. When the percentage of carbon dioxide in the blood increases greatly, as it does during hard work or play, the impulses from the automatic control center are stronger and more frequent. The breathing muscles respond to these command signals by contracting more vigorously and more frequently.

Now you have seen how your body is supplied with fuel and oxygen. But how are the two used to provide you with energy for work and play? Factories have central power plants where energy is produced. The energy is then distributed to the working parts of all the machines in the factory. But you are neither a factory nor a machine; you do not have a central power plant. Each of the trillions of cells of your body produces the energy it needs for its work. Each cell is its *own* power plant.

You will recall how the blood from the small intestine flows through the body, carrying digested food nutrients to all of the body's cells. The blood also carries oxygen to the cells. Each tiny air sac in the lungs is surrounded by a net of even tinier blood vessels. The blood that flows into each net comes from all parts of the body and is rich in carbon dioxide. Since both the air sacs and the blood vessels have extremely thin walls, the carbon dioxide from the blood vessels is able to pass into the air sacs, and oxygen from the air sacs is able to pass into the blood vessels. By this exchange, the blood is oxygenated, which means that the carbon dioxide is replaced with oxygen.

You get rid of the carbon dioxide as you exhale, and replenish the oxygen in the air sacs as you inhale.

The oxygen is carried from the lungs to all the cells of the body by a chemical in the red blood cells called hemoglobin. There are myriads of these round, microscopic red cells containing the oxygen-carrying hemoglobin. It is hemoglobin that gives blood its red color. When it combines with oxygen, which it does very readily, it is bright red; when it gives up its oxygen, which it does just as readily to the cells in the tissues that need it, the color becomes dark red.

In a furnace or in an engine, fuel and oxygen combine readily and rapidly, often with explosive force. This is oxidation. Energy in the form of light and intense heat is released.

Energy production under such conditions could not, of course, take place in the body. The process is indirect and complex. For example, when muscles work, as they do when you walk or lift a bundle, respiratory enzymes break down a substance made and stored in the muscle cells that we may call, for simplicity, ATP. This releases energy that enables the muscle fibers to contract, and the muscle to work.

The simple substances that result from this breakdown must be restored, rebuilt to form ATP, so that the muscle may continue to work. This restoration, too, requires energy. It is supplied by the oxidation of sugar. It is at this time that carbon dioxide and water are produced as waste products. Some heat is also produced.

You can get rid of the excess heat in your body in several ways. The evaporation of perspiration helps cool the body. The air that you exhale from the lungs is warm, and if oxidation in the body is increased, the breathing rate is similarly increased, and more heat is thrown off. When you rid the body of liquid waste from the bladder, you are also ridding it of excess heat.

Some of the heat is retained in the body. Your cells work best at a temperature of 98.6° Fahrenheit. If the temperature in the body rises above this normal point, as it does during a fast game of tennis or handball, the body acts to throw off more heat at a faster rate. A center in the brain regulates body temperature, under normal conditions. When the rate of oxidation in the cells is increased, the blood flowing through the tissues becomes warmer.

As the warm blood circulates through the heat-regulating center, nerve impulses are sent to organs that will help to get rid of the excess heat—the sweat glands, the breathing organs, and the bladder. Should the temperature of the body fall below normal, many muscles may start shivering, and their movements will generate a little body heat.

Your heat-regulating center works like a thermostat in a

home. Set at a comfortable 72°, for example, the heat-sensitive home thermostat will respond to a rise in temperature and will automatically cut the heat off until the temperature drops below 72°. Then it will turn the heat on again, thus maintaining a constant temperature. Your heat control center is a live thermostat.

You should know how to use a body thermometer to measure the temperature inside your body. The thermometer has markings on it that are spaced one degree apart, from 92° to 110° Fahrenheit. An arrow points to 98.6°, the normal body temperature. At one end of the thermometer is a bulb filled with mercury.

Before use, the thermometer should be wiped with alcohol, then rinsed with running water; or, if alcohol is not available, it can simply be rinsed thoroughly in running water. The thermometer is then held firmly by the end opposite the bulb and shaken sharply to get the mercury in the tube well below the arrow pointing to normal temperature.

If a mouth thermometer is used, it is placed under the tongue, and the lips are held closed for three minutes or more. A rectal thermometer is placed in the rectum for the same length of time. The thermometer is then removed and the temperature is read by noting the degree mark to which the mercury has risen in the column.

If the thermometer shows that your temperature is above 98.6°—your normal, healthful temperature—this means that your body's heat-regulating center is not working properly. You have a fever, and feel warm and flushed because of the excess body heat. This is a warning that something may be wrong in your body, something that prevents the heat-regulating center from controlling your temperature.

Since the respiratory system is constantly exposed to germ-laden air, it is not surprising that respiratory diseases, often accompanied by fever, are so common.

The most common ailment—one that plagues young and old alike—is a cold in the head, nose, and throat, caused by a variety of germs, bacteria, or viruses. You have germs in your nose and throat at all times, but you do not usually become ill if your resistance is high. When it is lowered—as when the body is chilled because of cold, dampness, or inadequate clothing; or when you are unduly tired or undernourished—the germs get a foothold in your body, multiply rapidly, and produce the poisons that give you the symptoms of a cold.

The best way to deal with a cold, then, is to *prevent* it. Obey the rules of healthful living. If you get plenty of rest, eat properly, and dress in accordance with weather conditions at all times, chances are that the germs that are always in your respiratory tract will not affect your health. Respiratory diseases often occur in epidemics—widespread infections; during such epidemics, it is wise to avoid crowds.

Should you catch a bad cold, however, resting in a warm bed will help the body to defeat this common enemy. When a persistent or high fever accompanies a cold, it is wise to consult a doctor, for what begins as a simple cold can become much more serious.

Germs from an infected throat may enter the middle

ears, as we learned earlier, through the Eustachian tubes that connect the two, resulting in a painful ear infection. If repeated, such infections may cause deafness. Germs can also work their way deeper into the respiratory tract and cause laryngitis, pharyngitis, bronchitis, influenza, or pneumonia.

For healthful respiration, a good air supply is essential. In the home, an air conditioner that maintains a healthful temperature of between 68° and 72°, and that ventilates, removes the excess moisture from, and filters the air can be very effective in aiding respiration. If you don't have an air conditioner, proper cross-ventilation through windows and doors should be maintained at all times. Since warm air rises, opening windows from the top will generally let out the used air. If the room has windows on opposite sides, opening one from the bottom and the other from the top will provide good air circulation.

The problem of improving the polluted air over our towns and cities is a more difficult one, which we will discuss in detail in a later chapter.

:five:

Your blood stream is a life stream

Do you know of a pump that can work throughout the day and night, day after day throughout the year, year after year throughout a lifetime, without stopping? You have such a pump. It is your heart.

Your heart is about the size of your closed fist. Its shape is more like that of a pear than like that shown on Valentine cards. If you will place your right fist on the lower half of your breastbone, pointing it to the left, you will locate the position of the heart in the chest. It is protected by the breastbone and the ribs.

The heart is made up of four parts, or chambers. On its upper, broad base are two flat (when empty) elastic sacs, the right and left auricles. Below these sacs are the right and left ventricles, which make up the bulk of the heart. The ventricles can hold no more blood than the auricles.

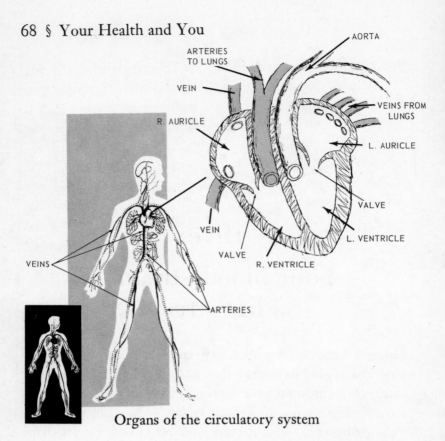

Organs of the circulatory system

Their much greater size is due to the thickness of their muscular walls, the left one being very much thicker than the right. Each auricle is separated from its connecting ventricle by a valve; and the right side of the heart is completely separated from the left side.

"Impure" blood that is laden with carbon dioxide is brought to the right auricle from all organs of the body (except the lungs) by two large blood tubes, veins. "Pure" blood that is rich in oxygen is brought to the left auricle from the lungs by four smaller veins. Thus the "pure" blood and the "impure" blood are kept apart in the heart.

When the auricles are filled, they contract, forcing the blood through the valves into the respective ventricles. Next the ventricles contract. The valves between the chambers are closed.

From the right ventricle the "impure" blood is carried by the lung artery to the lungs. Here it flows about the air sacs, where it is relieved of carbon dioxide while taking on oxygen. Now "purified," it returns to the left auricle.

Meantime, blood from the left ventricle has passed into the aorta, the largest artery of the body, an inch in diameter. This is purified blood that has come from the lungs, and it will be recirculated to all of the organs of the body, then returned to the right auricle.

The heart is really a double pump, the right side being for lung circulation and the left side for body circulation. The two circulations work together, of course; otherwise the circulatory system would not work at all. The two auricles contract at the same time, followed by the contraction of both ventricles. Such a cycle is called a heartbeat.

During normal activity, the heart of a girl or boy of your age group beats about eighty to ninety times a minute. The rate is somewhat higher for girls than for boys. It is greatly increased when you run, jump, or play an active game. At these times the heart responds quickly to the needs of the cells for more fuel and oxygen. The heart beats faster and harder to deliver a greater volume of blood to the tissues. It will do so, also, as a result of a deep emotion—when you feel very happy or very fearful, for example. The rate of the heartbeat is automatically controlled in the brain, as is the breathing rate.

The heart can withstand normal increased demands, but putting unnecessary strain on it is not healthful. That is why competitive athletic games are not encouraged or approved for girls and boys between ten and twelve. In many young people of this age, the heart does not yet function perfectly, and undue strain may be put on it. Physical and emotional strains can also pile up and cause damage that in later years may impair the effective work of the heart.

You have no doubt had a doctor listen to your heart through his stethoscope, which amplifies the sound the heart makes as it beats. These sounds give him information about how well your heart is working. He may hear a murmur. This is caused by the vibration of valves that do not close properly. Such a heart does not work efficiently because some of the blood leaks back into the chamber from which it is being pumped. Such a condition very often corrects itself after a time. A doctor may prescribe limited exercise or activity for a youngster with a leaky heart valve.

Heart diseases are not common or serious health problems at your age. But they are principal causes of death in older people.

Good health habits formed now and continued as you grow up will help to insure you a healthier heart for a longer life. These habits include regular exercises that you may continue into adult life; a wholesome mixed and balanced diet; freedom from mental and emotional problems; and sufficient rest and recreation.

The blood that the heart pumps appears to be a liquid. It is, however, 45 percent solids. The liquid part, 55 percent, is called plasma. The solids are two kinds of cells, red and white corpuscles. The blood is a tissue whose cells are not held together, but float in the plasma. When you are fully grown you will have about ten pints of blood in your body.

The red corpuscles are by far the more numerous, about five to six million in a single drop of blood. From this you may well imagine that they are extremely small. Red corpuscles are round, flat, and hollowed on both sides. They are short-lived, lasting about three months, and are constantly being replaced by new ones that are formed in the red marrow of bones.

Red corpuscles give your blood its color, and it is the hemoglobin that makes them red. This chemical, you will recall, is the oxygen carrier of the body. As blood circulates around the air sacs in the lungs, oxygen combines readily with the hemoglobin in the corpuscles. Later, in the tissues, the combination breaks up as readily, with the oxygen passing into the cells.

In order to make hemoglobin, your body needs iron. Some is saved from the worn-out corpuscles, but more is continually added from the food that you eat—particularly green vegetables, red meats, and liver.

Girls and boys with pale, sallow complexions may suffer from anemia, a shortage of iron in the blood. This may be accompanied by a lack of energy because the blood does not deliver to the tissues enough oxygen for energy production. If adding iron-rich foods to the diet does not improve the condition, medical help should be sought.

The white corpuscles are irregularly shaped, larger than the red ones, and less numerous, there being about six to eight thousand in a single drop of blood. They are able to leave the blood stream by squeezing between the cells that make up the walls of the tiniest blood vessels.

When the skin is broken by a cut or a bruise, white corpuscles quickly gather at the site to repel the invading germs. They are able to eat and destroy them. The pus that forms at the site of an infected wound is made up largely of dead germs and corpuscles.

When you get a small cut, scratch, or bruise you should wash it, then apply an antiseptic. This is a chemical that prevents or stops the growth of bacteria. Then you should cover the wound with a sterile bandage—one that has been wrapped and sealed, then heated to kill any germs that may have gotten on the gauze. The bandage will keep out other invading germs. In this way you help the white corpuscles at the site of the wound, and it should then heal without infection.

As you will remember, blood is made up partly of solids—the corpuscles—and partly of liquid—the plasma. Blood plasma is a very complex liquid. It is nine parts water. The tenth part includes many substances, and both the kinds and the amounts change as the blood circulates. Digested nutrients are absorbed into the plasma as it flows through the small intestine; these nutrients are absorbed from the plasma as it circulates through the tissues. Cell wastes enter the plasma at the tissues and are removed from it as the blood circulates through the organs that rid the body of them.

The plasma also carries substances called antibodies that protect the body against invading germs or the poisons that they produce in the body. The antibodies are made by tissues, then pass into the blood. These protective bodies may also be produced by an animal (a horse, for example), and then injected into our bodies.

Chemicals from certain glands also enter the plasma and travel throughout the body. These chemicals help to regulate the work of various organs.

Since active organs such as muscles produce a great deal of heat, the blood passing through them is warmed. Then, as the blood circulates through cooler parts of the body, it gives up heat to them. When an excessive amount of heat is produced, the heat-regulating center in the brain sends an increased flow of blood to the skin, the lungs, and the bladder. Through these organs much of the excess heat is thrown off. Thus, the plasma helps to regulate body temperature.

What stops the blood from escaping from even a small cut? If given a chance, it forms a clot. A chemical in the plasma forms fibers at the cut tissues, making a sort of net in which the corpuscles become trapped. This tangle of fibers and cells is the clot that plugs the blood vessels. As it dries it becomes a hard scab. This scab remains firmly on the cut or scraped surface until the tissues beneath it have healed and new cells have replaced the injured ones; then it falls off. If you become impatient and pull off the scab, bleeding starts again, followed by another clot, then another scab.

Large cuts that bleed so freely that a clot cannot form

usually require medical care. But the loss of blood may be so great that the bleeding will have to be controlled until a doctor arrives. (First-aid measures will be discussed in a later chapter.)

Blood, you will recall, leaves the heart through arteries. The largest, the aorta, carries blood from the left ventricle to all the organs of the body, except the lungs. Near its exit from the heart, branches from the aorta pass to the head, the shoulders, and the arms. The aorta then makes a loop and extends down through the trunk. Along its way, branches of it go off to the organs of the chest and the abdomen. Near the lower end of the abdomen the aorta divides into two main branches, one of which extends down each leg.

In an organ the main artery divides many times, forming increasingly smaller branches that reach every part of the organ. The very smallest arteries divide to form a net of microscopic blood vessels called capillaries, which surround clusters of cells. It is through the extremely thin walls of the capillaries that oxygen, nutrients, and chemicals pass from the blood to the tissues, and useful cell products, as well as cell wastes, pass into the blood. You have already read about such interchange in the air sacs of the lungs and in the villi of the small intestine.

The capillaries of a net unite to form a very small vein, and it, in turn, unites with others to form larger veins. This continues until there is one principal vein that carries off the blood from each organ. Such blood vessels join one of two main veins: one from the upper part of the body (head, neck, arms, shoulders); the other from the lower

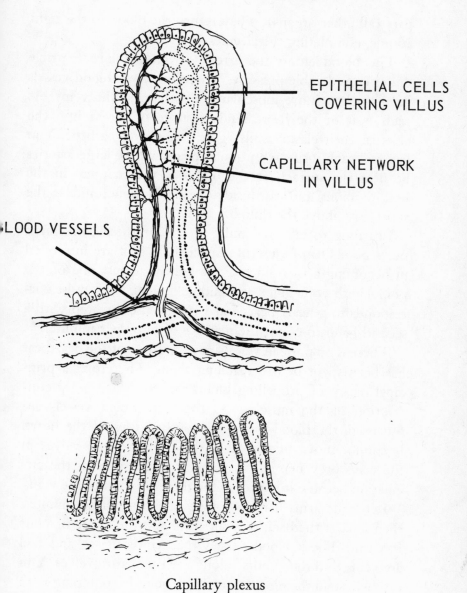

EPITHELIAL CELLS
COVERING VILLUS

CAPILLARY NETWORK
IN VILLUS

LOOD VESSELS

Capillary plexus

part (all other organs). They return the blood to the right auricle, completing the circuit.

The blood enters the arteries from the left ventricle under considerable pressure. Therefore these blood vessels have thicker, more muscular walls than do the veins. As each beat of the heart sends a surge of blood into the arteries, their elastic walls "give," or stretch, a little. You can feel each surge as a pulse at places where large arteries lie near the surface of the body—at the temples; in the hollow about midway inside the collar bone; and at the wrist, just above the thumb.

Learning to take the pulse at one of these convenient pulse points can be useful, especially if you are interested in becoming a first aider. Press lightly against one of the points with your index and middle fingers. Each pulse corresponds to a heart beat, and you can use a watch with a second hand to count the number of beats per minute.

There is no pulse in veins since the force of the heartbeat has been spent before reaching them. Therefore, a principal means of propelling blood through them is by contraction of the muscles. As the thin-walled vessels are squeezed, the blood in them is pushed toward the heart. It cannot move in the other direction because valves in the veins prevent such movement. Exercise helps the circulation because it improves the flow of blood in the veins.

Let your arms hang by your sides for a few minutes, then look at the back of your hand and the inside of your forearm. Those blood vessels that you can see and feel are veins, and the "knots" along their paths are valves. You can help send the blood along these veins by pumping with your hands, opening and closing them vigorously a dozen times or so; or by raising your arms above your head so that the blood may drain toward the heart.

There is a saying that one is as old as one's arteries. Sick arteries affect twice as many older people as do all other diseases together. The walls of the vessels harden, losing their elasticity, and as a result one of them may burst from the pressure of the blood within. If one ruptures in the head, a clot may form and press on an area of the brain that controls the movement of the muscles in certain parts of the body. When this happens, the muscles become paralyzed. Sometimes the condition is temporary. The clot will be absorbed, the pressure relieved, and the function of the muscles restored. But in other cases, the paralysis may be permanent. Such a rupture, causing temporary or permanent paralysis, is called a stroke. A massive one may be fatal.

You will keep your arteries younger longer if you form good health habits now. Briefly, they are: regular exercise, sufficient rest and recreation, freedom from mental and emotional stresses, and a good mixed and balanced diet. Many doctors recommend reducing the use of fats of animal origin (butter and bacon, for example) as one grows older. One more caution: watch your weight as you become adult. There is a tendency to eat more and exercise less. Excess weight may be a burden to the organs of circulation.

Another type of circulation in the body starts at the capillaries. Plasma oozes out of them and white corpuscles squeeze out between the cells that make up their walls.

The mixture of plasma and white corpuscles that results is lymph, sometimes called "white" blood. Lymph surrounds both the cells and the capillary net that enmeshes each cluster of them. Hence, all the materials that are exchanged between the capillaries and the cells—oxygen, carbon dioxide, nutrients, wastes, and chemicals—must pass through the lymph.

The contraction of muscles pushes the lymph along through thin-walled tubes. Smaller tubes unite to form larger ones; the larger ones unite, finally, to form the large lymphatic duct that joins a large vein near the right side of the heart. Thus the lymph is restored to the blood stream, and the lymph circulation is completed.

If you have had a blister that opened, you have seen lymph. It is the whitish liquid that fills the space between the top skin and the underlying skin when the two become separated by a burn, or as a result of rubbing.

If one loses a little blood from a small cut or a brief nosebleed, the body soon makes up the loss of plasma and corpuscles. But should one lose a great deal as a result of a serious wound or severe hemorrhage, a doctor would have to replace it from a blood bank.

Many healthy people donate a pint of blood to a hospital or to the Red Cross. The blood is kept under refrigeration in sterile, sealed containers until it is needed in an emergency. Then the doctor may use whole blood containing both plasma and corpuscles, or he may use just the plasma. When the whole blood or plasma is introduced into a patient's vein, this is a blood transfusion.

The doctor does not draw just any blood from the bank—it must be the right type. It has been found that each person in the world has one of four distinct types of blood. This has nothing to do with one's race or nationality; all four types are found among all peoples.

Blood from different people with the same type may be mixed, transfused, without difficulty. Though some bloods of *different* types can also be mixed successfully, there are other types that cannot. The red corpuscles may stick together in clumps, clogging the vessels of the patient.

Since a doctor must know the blood type of the patient and of the blood donor before he gives a transfusion, you should ask your doctor what type of blood you have. In an emergency, it could save time if you knew your type, without having to have your blood tested.

Your blood stream delivers to your cells the materials that they need for their healthful activity. It also maintains a body temperature in which the cells can work, and removes from their environment materials that would be injurious to them. In short, your blood stream is your life stream.

:six:

Maintaining a healthy internal environment

When the conditions in your external environment—your everyday world—are safe and pleasant, you can enjoy being in it and can function happily and efficiently.

The cells of your body also require favorable conditions in their environment in order to work effectively. These conditions, as you have learned, include a food supply, an oxygen supply, suitable temperature, and protection against germs. Now you will see how another essential condition for the cells' effective functioning is achieved—the removal of the waste products of cell activity.

In the chapter on the respiratory system, you read how the cells produce a waste product, carbon dioxide. This waste product is removed from the cells' environment by the blood, and from the body by the lungs.

As they work, the cells produce another waste product,

urea. This, too, is removed from the cells' environment by·
the blood, and is removed from the body by special organs
of excretion (waste disposal)—the kidneys and the skin.

If you will make two fists, then place them behind you
in the small of your back, one on either side of your backbone, they will lie above the two kidneys. The kidneys
are bean-shaped, like the beans that are called kidney beans.

Each kidney includes many millions of microscopic cups
attached to long, twisted microscopic tubes. Blood comes
to each cup through a small artery, then flows through a
net of capillaries within each cup, and leaves through a
small vein. The blood comes to the kidney laden with urea,
uric acid, and other products that are to be removed from
the body.

The kidneys' tiny cups and the attached tubes are not
simple strainers. They are able to remove from the blood
not only urea, but also an excess of water, sugar, some
amino acids, minerals (sodium and potassium, for example), and several other body wastes.

The kidneys are further able to select certain amounts
of the products for removal—more at one time, less at another—according to the conditions in the body. From each
kidney comes a liquid made up mostly of water, with the
other products dissolved in it. This is urine. It passes into
two rather thick, muscular tubes, the ureters, where
muscular contractions squeeze it along into the bladder, an
elastic, muscular bag.

Urine is about 95 percent water. Half of the remaining
5 percent is urea. As the bladder fills, tension builds up
until the urine is voided from the body through the

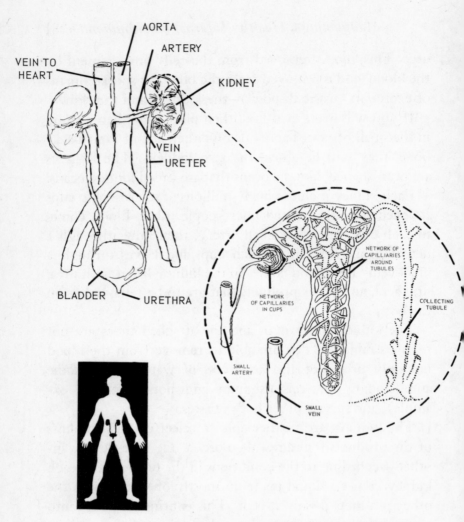

The excretory (urinary) system. A single excretory unit

urethra. The amount that is given off in a day varies according to the amount of activity. On a normal day one may eliminate as much as a quart; when one has played hard and long the amount may be more than doubled.

The urine of a patient is very useful to a doctor in determining what may be wrong in the body. He makes a urine analysis to find out what substances are in it and the amount of each. For example, the analysis may show that there is an excess of sugar in the urine. If the patient has eaten a lot of candy, the kidneys are probably just throwing off the excess sugar—a temporary condition. The doctor will insist on checking the patient's urine again, however, and if an excess of sugar occurs in follow-up analyses, he will suspect that the patient has diabetes, a disease in which sugar is not properly stored and used in the body. If a larger than normal amount of a certain protein, albumin, is found, the doctor might suspect trouble in the kidneys themselves. And there is much more that may be learned from a urine analysis. That is why doctors so often ask for a specimen.

Urea, water, and a few other salt wastes are excreted by the skin. While it is spread thin over the entire surface of the body, the skin is really an organ. What is generally regarded as the skin is really a layer of compressed, dead skin cells. This is the epidermis, a covering, protective layer over the live skin beneath it.

Lying beneath the epidermis is the live skin, the dermis. This is the pink skin that you find under a blister or under a scab before new epidermis has formed. In the dermis are found many capillaries, sense organs of touch, nerves, hair follicles, oil glands, and sweat glands.

A game of tennis or handball or any other fast game leaves you drenched with perspiration. A hot, humid day does the same. Then you know that your sweat glands are

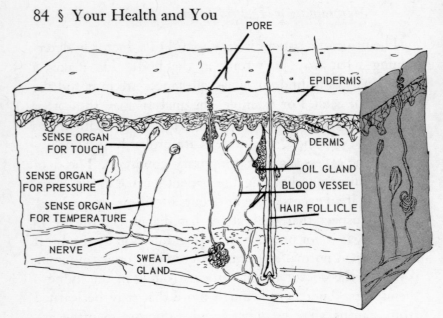

Structure of the skin; a very highly magnified section

at work. But they are always at work, causing you to perspire all the time. You are not aware of it on a cool day or when you are quiet, because the perspiration comes out slowly, and either is absorbed by your clothes, or evaporates.

Millions of these microscopic sweat glands are found in the dermis all over the surface of the body. Each one consists of a coiled tube, with a short tube extending from it to an opening (a pore) in the epidermis. The coiled section is surrounded by capillaries. As the blood flows through them, the wastes are absorbed into the sweat glands and pass to the surface through the pores. When you exercise or when you are in a warm place, your body automatically sends a greater volume of blood to the skin, making you look flushed and increasing the excretion of perspiration.

Perspiration (sweat) is 99 percent water. You lose a pint or more on an ordinary day; four or more times as much on a hot day; sixteen or more times as much playing an active game on a hot day. In addition, you lose about a quart a day in urine; a pint or more as water vapor from the lungs; and a little in the food waste from the large intestine. You replace this water loss with the beverages you drink, and also from the food that you eat.

You have a built-in reminder to take water. It is the feeling of thirst resulting from the drying of the membrane that lines the mouth and throat. If you have read adventure stories about men who have been lost in a desert, you know that excessive loss of water—called dehydration—can be very serious.

When you are sweating, heat from the skin changes the liquid sweat into water vapor (a process known as evaporation). This cools the skin and helps to regulate the body temperature.

But while the water evaporates, the urea and salts remain on the skin. And as you enter your teen years, the oil glands in the skin will become more active. Though this oil helps to keep the skin smooth and soft, an excess makes the skin look greasy. The oil mixes with the sweat on the skin, and some of the mixture is absorbed by the underclothing, while some remains on the skin. If sweat and oil are allowed to remain on the skin, bacteria will act on the mixture, resulting in body odor.

Though many remedies are advertised for the elimination of body odors, they will not be effective for any length of time if you do not practice the simple, healthful habit of bathing daily—several times, if necessary, in warm weather. You should also change your underclothing frequently.

A warm bath with soap removes from your skin the urea, salts, oil, bacteria, dust, and dead epidermal cells that constantly scale off. Moreover, if the temperature of the water is a little above that inside the body, the effect is soothing. A cool or cold shower following a warm bath improves the circulation.

Cleanliness of the hair and scalp is also important in personal hygiene. Oil that is produced in glands in the skin of the scalp mixes with the dust from the air and with dead scales from the surface of the scalp. The hair and scalp should be washed thoroughly with soap and water once a week, more if necessary, to rid them of this mixture.

An inflammation of the skin of the scalp may result in excessive scaling—dandruff. If frequent shampooing does not improve the condition, it would be wiser to consult a skin doctor than to experiment with advertised dandruff remedies.

The hands perspire, too. Since you use them to handle all kinds of germ-laden objects, they should be washed frequently with soap and water—certainly before handling food that is to be taken into the mouth.

As you enter your teens, some of you may develop acne, a skin condition caused, basically, by changes that take place in the body at this time. One of the results is the increase of the production of oil by the glands in the skin.

The openings of these glands may become clogged, and the oil hardened and mixed with dirt, causing blackheads. If they become infected and inflamed, pimples result.

For acne, as for body odors, there are many advertised remedies. If the condition is very severe or very troublesome, it should be treated by a doctor. Normally, proper hygiene will control and sometimes reduce the extent of the outbreak. The face should be washed three or four times a day with plenty of soap and water. Don't use a brush or rough face cloth or towel, for they may spread the infection. Rest, and outdoor exercise in the sun for an hour or two a day will also help lessen the symptoms of acne.

There are several don'ts. Do not squeeze blackheads or pimples, as this may spread infection. Avoid eating chocolates, nuts, peanut butter, fried foods, and other fatty foods, as these may promote the production of oil by glands in the skin. With time, patience, and hygienic care you will outgrow the condition of acne and will have no blemishes.

Eruptions and rashes that may appear on the skin of the face, arms, and body may be symptoms of serious disturbances in the internal environment. Each kind is unique, the symptom of a particular disease. Thus chicken pox, German measles, measles, scarlet fever, and smallpox each produces a rash that is readily and clearly identifiable. Such diseases are more common among young children, but they may affect girls and boys of your age group, and even adults.

Such rashes are unpleasant and unsightly; they may be very annoying and irritating, especially when they itch. Moreover, they may be infectious. A suspicious eruption should be seen by a doctor, who can identify it. He will treat the cause, which may have serious effects in the body. It is unwise to try self-treatment.

The liver, the largest gland in the body, is another essential guardian of the internal environment. The blood that has absorbed digested nutrients in the small intestine passes through the liver on its way to the heart. Liver cells remove and store as animal starch some of the excess sugar; in addition, they convert some of the excess amino acids into animal starch and store it; some excess amino acids are changed into urea that is later removed from the blood and from the body by the kidneys and the skin; and, finally, the liver cells can make harmless some poisons that may have gotten into the blood.

The digestive system disposes of the waste that results from food digestion. The respiratory system removes from the body the wastes of energy production. The excretory system removes from the cells' environment any other wastes that may contaminate it, and impair the work of the cells.

:seven:

Your sense organs are your sentinels

How do you become aware of your environment—to enjoy its pleasures and to avoid its dangers? Your sense organs are your sentinels. They alert you to what is going on about you and within you.

Your radio or television antenna receives "signals" of electromagnetic waves from the air. They are changed into sound or pictures, or both, in the receiving set. Your sense organs receive "stimuli" from your surroundings. These stimuli become sensations of sight, hearing, smell, taste, touch, and others.

Your eyes are your chief sentinels. Light waves that originate in the sun, an electric lamp, or other light source strike objects in your surroundings, such as a building, an automobile, or people. The waves bounce off the objects; that is, they are reflected. If they enter your eyes, they are the stimuli (the signals) that enable you to see the objects.

Your eyes are set in deep sockets in front of your skull. This gives them some protection so that most blows at the eye, accidental or on purpose, strike the area about the socket. This is how one gets a "black eye." The color results from the blood's flowing out of the many broken capillaries in the skin.

The eyelids also protect the delicate eyeballs. They close automatically as particles approach. The eyelashes also help to catch dust particles.

Tears flow constantly over the eyeball to keep it moist and to wash away offending dust particles. If a particle is especially irritating, the tears flow more freely. Should a particle become embedded on the inside of a lid or on the eyeball, it may have to be washed out with an eyecup of boiled water or it may have to be removed with a bit of sterile cotton or gauze and then bathed with boiled water. You should not rub the eye to remove an offending particle as this could injure the delicate membrane that lines the lid, or even the eyeball itself. The eyes are too precious to be tampered with.

You may close your eyelids voluntarily, as you do when you wink or go to sleep. You open your eyes when you raise your lids. Then light rays that are reflected from objects in your surroundings pass through the transparent window, the cornea, in the front of the eyeball.

The amount of light that enters the eye is controlled automatically by the iris, the colored disk that you see in your eye. Its tiny muscles make the opening in it (called the pupil) larger in dim light and smaller in bright light.

NEAR SIGHTED EYE   FAR SIGHTED EYE

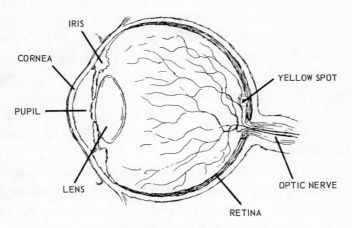

The structure of the eye

The color of the iris has nothing to do with its function.

From the iris the light rays then pass through the lens and fall on the retina, the back wall of the eyeball. The cornea and the lens gather the light rays so that they come to a focus on a small, yellow spot on the retina. This is the area of clearest vision and of color vision.

In the retina, and especially in the yellow spot, there are many thousands of nerve cells that are sensitive to light. The light rays are the stimuli (signals) that start a current, or a nerve impulse, to the brain. It travels along the optic (seeing) nerve. The image that you see is actually recorded —seen—in the brain rather than in the eye. A person can be blinded by a blow on the back of the head where the seeing center is located, although the eye itself is uninjured.

The lens of your eye can adjust to enable you to see objects that are either near or far. But you cannot see both clearly at the same time. Hold this book in front of you so that you can see and read the print on the page. Can you, at the same time, see clearly a picture on the wall beyond the book? Keep the book before you at the same distance, but look at the picture. Can you, at the same time, read the print on the page? Very tiny muscles pull the lens flat for far vision and relax to make it thicker for near vision. The eye muscles do this automatically, in a process called accommodation.

Do you have to hold this book closer than fifteen inches from your eyes to read it easily? Or do you have to hold it at arm's length—more than fifteen inches—to do so? You may be nearsighted in the first case, farsighted in the second. In nearsighted persons the eyes do not accommodate by flattening the lenses sufficiently. In farsighted persons the lenses do not accommodate by becoming thick enough for near vision. On the other hand, the trouble may be caused by the shape of the eyeballs. In a nearsighted eye the eyeball is more or less elongated; in a farsighted eye it is more or less shortened. Whatever the cause, the result is that the light rays do not focus as they should on the yellow spot in the retina.

In either case, seeing can be improved even though the defect cannot be corrected. Eyeglasses are the remedy. Nearsighted persons are fitted with lenses that spread the light rays before the rays enter the eyes. Farsighted persons are fitted with lenses that gather the light rays before they enter the eyes. The fitting should be done by an oculist (eye doctor). An optometrist grinds the lenses and fits them to the patient according to the oculist's prescription.

As you look at this printed page does one part appear darker and clearer than another? This is caused by a defect of the eye that is called astigmatism. The surface of the cornea or of the lens may not be perfectly rounded, with the result that the light rays are not focused equally. This defect may also be remedied by properly fitted lenses.

Instead of eyeglasses, some people prefer to wear invisible contact lenses. These are corrective in the same way that the lenses of eyeglasses are, but are worn directly on the eyeball!.

Crossed eyes—another common eye defect—cannot be remedied so easily. Each eyeball has three pairs of muscles attached to it, enabling you to move your eyes in the many ways that you do. Sometimes a child is born with one of a pair of muscles weaker than its opposing one. The eyeball is pulled out of alignment, and a crossed eye results. One or both eyes may have the defect.

Vision is impaired because the two eyes do not see an object in the same way. Sometimes a doctor tries to correct this condition with exercises for the weak muscle or muscles. It is usually corrected, though, by surgery. Many eye doctors now believe that the correction must be made in the first year of the infant's life, for the sight path from the eye to the seeing center is fixed at that time. If the correction is done later, the person's appearance will be improved, but the vision will have been impaired.

Poor lighting causes eye strain and makes reading difficult. You are reading this page by the light that is reflected from it to your eyes. Is there any direct light coming into your eyes at the same time? If so, it makes reading less comfortable. Your pupils are more contracted than they should be for the reflected light to enter easily. If you are reading by daylight, it should be coming over a shoulder onto the book, so that you are not facing the light. If you are reading by artificial light, the principle is the same. The preferred type of lamp is one with a dark shade that spreads the light evenly on the page, while keeping it out of your eyes.

Do you recall reading that vitamin A helps you to see in dim light? The cells of the retina use this vitamin to make a chemical that enables them to do so.

Just as your eyes are your sight sentinels, your ears are your sound sentinels. Even as you sit reading this book you are aware of many sounds to which you do not pay attention: the ticking of a clock, the shuffling of feet, voices, cars passing in the street, doors closing, and many others. We accept these sounds as part of our environment. Indeed, we miss a familiar sound if it stops suddenly.

Sounds are produced by the vibrations of a body as it moves back and forth very rapidly. Vibrations may be made, for example, by the string of a violin, the clanging of a trash can, or the vocal cords in the voice box. The vibrating body causes the air about it to vibrate, producing a succession of air waves.

The more rapidly the body vibrates, the shorter the resulting waves are and the higher and shriller the resulting sounds. We cannot hear extremely short sound waves.

Your ears are sound-wave receivers. The part that you see, the outer ears, are really more ornamental than useful. However, the canals that lead in from them are important in hearing. The sound waves travel along the canals to thin membranes that are stretched across their ends. These membranes are the eardrums.

Tiny hairs in the canal catch dust that comes into the ear with the air. If the wax forms in large amounts, a soft cotton swab may be used to remove it. In rare cases the wax may become hardened. If this happens to you, you should see a doctor, for such a hard mass may impair your hearing.

Hearing begins at the eardrums. Extremely thin and highly sensitive, the eardrums vibrate readily when sound waves reach them. Their vibrations vary in accordance with the differences in the length of the sound waves that strike them.

The eardrum separates the ear canal from a very small space called the middle ear. Within this space there are three tiny bones that are attached to one another in succession. The free end of the first bone is attached to the eardrum; the free end of the third bone fits into a window in a snail-shaped bone that is the inner ear. The second bone connects the first and the third ones.

The inner ear is called the cochlea. It is very small, only one-third of an inch across its base and one-fifth of an inch high. Its structure is that of a coiled tube about an inch and a quarter long and about one-sixteenth of an inch in diameter. Along its length there are about twenty-four thousand "hair" cells. These vary in length from $1/15$ of

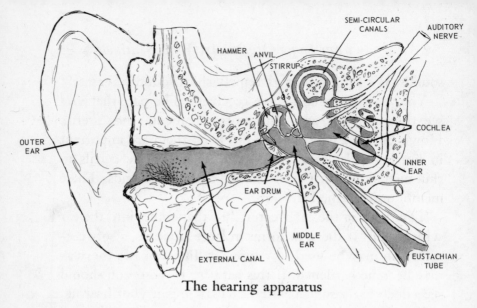

The hearing apparatus

an inch to 1/170 of an inch. We may think of the cochlea as the transformer of the hearing organs. Within it the sound waves (signals) are changed into nerve impulses.

While the outer ears are quite large, the actual organs of hearing are extremely small. They are encased in the hard bones of the skull at the side of the head, behind the outer ears.

The vibrations of the eardrum are passed along to the bones of the middle ear. They, in turn, pass the vibrations to a fluid that fills the tube of the cochlea. The hair cells pick up the vibrations and pass them on to nerve cells. Now, as nerve impulses, they are carried to the brain through the auditory (hearing) nerve. The sensation of hearing takes place in the brain.

Not all girls and boys hear equally well. For example, some pupils cannot hear a teacher if they are seated in the rear of the classroom. For this reason, many schools

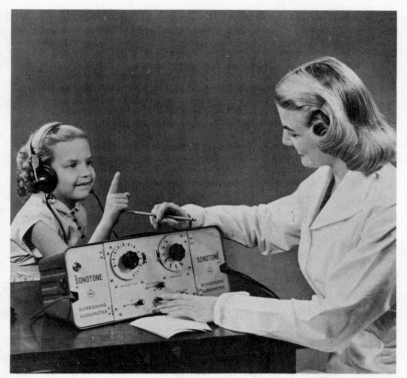

The girl's hearing is being tested with an audiometer. She raises her finger as a signal to the tester, according to the instructions for the test. The tester can then tell by reading the dials on the audiometer how well the girl hears a particular sound.

test the pupils' hearing every few years. It may become impaired.

The testing is done with an audiometer. This is like a phonograph or tape-recorder with earphones. The record or tape reproduces sounds of different pitch, from very low to very high. The operator of the audiometer can control the intensity of the sound, from loud to soft. The pupil being tested listens through one ear at a time as the audiometer tests the keenness of hearing of each ear. It can also discover if there has been any loss of hearing of high or of low tones.

Many people, young and old, suffer some hearing loss. The cause may often be traced to some childhood disease, perhaps no more serious than repeated sore throats. Germs may get into the middle ear from the throat through the tube that connects them. Thus the bones of the middle ear may become damaged. Another common ear injury results from the use of something sharp, such as a toothpick or hairpin, to remove wax from the canal. The eardrum may be punctured in the process.

People who suffer a serious loss of hearing may often be helped with a hearing aid. This is, essentially, a small microphone that is usually placed in the canal. The microphone, powered by a battery, amplifies the sound waves. If the hearing loss is due to damage to the tiny bones of the middle ear, surgery may often correct the condition.

The cochlea is part of a larger bone that includes, also, three semicircular bones or canals. They are the sense organs for balance. Although they are attached near the cochlea, the sense of balance and the sense of hearing are altogether independent of each other.

It is not known just how the semicircular canals work. But nerve impulses pass from them to a special part of the brain; and from that part of the brain, the center for balance, they pass to muscles. The sense organs for balance and the center for balance together coordinate the many muscles that enable you to stand erect; to recover and straighten yourself when you have lost your balance; and to get your bearings after a somersault, spin, or roll.

The roll and pitch of a boat on windswept waters or the tossing of a plane in bumpy air upsets the sense of balance of many people. They become more or less nauseous at the same time. This is seasickness or airsickness. On a long boat trip many get their "sea legs" in a few days; they recover their sense of balance. Air trips are shorter, so that the victims usually recover when they get their "land legs" when they arrive once more on firm ground.

You may sometimes see a person who has drunk too much alcohol stagger along unsteadily. Alcohol affects the vision as well as the organs of balance so that the person cannot control his posture, his gait, or his direction.

When you sit down to eat, three senses help you to enjoy your meal and, therefore, to digest it better—sight (which has already been discussed), taste, and smell.

Taste and smell are often confused. For example, do you taste or smell a piece of onion, a piece of garlic, a piece of ripe cheese? Tiny clusters of cells that are sensitive to sweet or sour, salty or bitter flavors are found on the tongue. These are the taste buds. The cells that are sensitive to odors are found in the nostrils. Odors may reach them from the throat as well as from the outside air.

You can taste foods only when they are in liquid form, in solution. Check this by these simple experiments on yourself. Wipe your tongue dry with a clean paper tissue, then sprinkle some grains of sugar on it. They will not taste sweet. Put some grains of sugar in a few drops of water, then place them on the tongue, and you will detect the sweet taste. You may try similar experiments with grains of salt, particles of a crushed sour lemon drop, or finely ground coffee grains. Now you know another reason for mixing your food thoroughly with saliva while you keep it in the mouth—you get more taste from it.

You may also do experiments to discover the difference between taste and smell. Holding your nostrils closed with the fingers of one hand, place a slice of onion on your wet tongue. Try also a sliver of garlic, then a piece of ripe cheese. You do not taste any of them. If you repeat the experiments with your nostrils open, you will recognize their "flavors." They are really their odors.

The senses of taste and of smell are sentinels, although not as crucial as are those of sight and sound in making one aware of the environment. Taste and smell enable you to relish the flavor of food and to enjoy the fragrance of flowers. But people have eaten toadstools, mistaking them for mushrooms, because they were unable to taste the deadly poison in them; and have eaten spoiled meat that contained a poison equally as deadly. While the nerve endings in the nostrils can detect some harmful gases, they are not able to pick up the deadly carbon monoxide from the exhaust of automobile engines. You will have to use other information, besides that supplied by the senses of taste and smell, to insure the safety of your food supply and air supply.

More reliable sentinels are the many thousands of nerve endings in the dermis of your skin. Some of them are sensitive to heat, some to cold. Others are sensitive to pressure, still others to pain. Each of these sensations is received at different spots located all over the body. Together, they make up what is generally called the sense of "touch."

Since most of the skin of the body is usually covered with clothing, except for the face and the hands, it is through the skin of the hands that we get most of our information about the feel of things. You test the temperature of bath water with your finger. If your mother suspects that you have fever, she first feels your forehead with the palm of her hand. On a warm day you feel a bottle of soda pop to find out if it is cold enough. The pressure points in your skin tell you whether an object is as smooth as a baby's skin or as rough as sandpaper; as hard as a rock or as soft as dough. They will tell you, also, if a knife is sharp; but when you press too hard, the pain spots will tell you that you have gone too far.

In short, your sense organs make you aware of your environment, give you information about it, enable you to enjoy it, and guard you against dangers in it.

But you also have internal sentinels to alert you to conditions within the body. For example, when you have overeaten, you "feel full." Should you have indigestion as a result of it, you will have "a pain in the stomach." The sensation of pain is useful not only as a warning that something is wrong, but also in locating the site of the trouble. It should not be "killed" with a pain killer; instead, its cause should be found and corrected.

Sense organs receive stimuli—of light and sound, of smell and taste, of heat and cold, of pressure and pain. From the sense organs messages, or nerve impulses, are carried to the brain. They become sensations in the brain, and from there appropriate action is directed.

The brain is not only the center for sensations. It is concerned with everything that goes on in the body. You will learn about it in the next chapter.

:eight:
Your body organs work
as a team

At this moment, as you sit reading this book, you appear to be quite inactive. Yet muscles are working to support your head and back as you sit upright. The muscles of your arm and hand hold the book, and from time to time they turn the pages. As your eyes move from left to right and from line to line, you may shift your position now and again. These movements are all voluntary, meaning that they are under the control of your will. You may stop reading and do something else.

As you read, you breathe, and your heart beats in steady rhythm. The pupils of your eyes become larger or smaller as the light changes. These and other activities over which you do not appear to have control go on in your body continually. They are, indeed, involuntary actions, but they are not without control.

All the activities of the body are controlled, either voluntarily or involuntarily. That is, they are controlled consciously (with your awareness), or unconsciously (without it). They are, moreover, coordinated. You are a large organization, made up of trillions of cells, and you have a control system that insures effective cooperation of all the cells. Coordination and control are supplied by the nervous system, assisted by certain glands. The brain is the center for these functions.

Nerve impulses from sense organs become sensations in the brain. These sensations give you the information that makes you aware of conditions in your external environment and in your body. Nerve impulses from the brain carry orders to the organs of the body. Information is filed in the brain; this is your memory. In the brain, too, problems are solved, and ideas are born.

This vital and sensitive organ has maximum security, being encased in the skull and completely protected by hard bone. It requires a hard blow to fracture the skull, but it can happen. The crack may mend without permanent injury to the brain or to any organ controlled by it. If, however, the broken bone presses upon some areas of the brain, the result may be a loss of function in some organ or organs.

The largest part of the brain is the cerebrum. It includes two equal sections, the hemispheres, meaning "half" spheres. The surface of the cerebrum is deeply furrowed. Behind and just below the cerebrum is the cerebellum; and below this is the still smaller medulla. Some people think of the cerebrum as the brain, but all three parts are necessary in controlling and coordinating the work of the organs of the body.

Brains vary in size. When a girl is fully grown, her brain will weigh from thirty-one to fifty-eight ounces; that of a grown boy will weigh from thirty-five to sixty-six ounces. This variation is due to the generally larger skull size of the male, and is not related to intelligence. Evidence that brain size is not related to intelligence is found in the fact that the largest brain on record belonged to an idiot, and one of the smallest to a genius.

The brain is made up of cells called neurons. These special cells have multiple branches that enable the neurons to make numerous interconnections, like so many electric circuits.

The cerebrum is the center for sensations. Seeing, hearing, feeling, tasting, smelling, and the sensations from the internal organs are all experienced in special areas of the cerebrum. Any injury to such an area results in the loss of a particular sensation, even though the sense organ itself is uninjured.

The contraction and relaxation of the voluntary muscles—those that are attached to the bones—are controlled in the motor areas of the cerebrum. Injury to a particular motor area may result in loss of function, or paralysis, of particular muscles or of an entire limb or part of a limb.

Still other areas of the cerebrum are concerned with memory, thinking, and reasoning. And all the areas of the cerebrum are interconnected. It has infinitely more interconnections than a computer (electronic brain) has circuits.

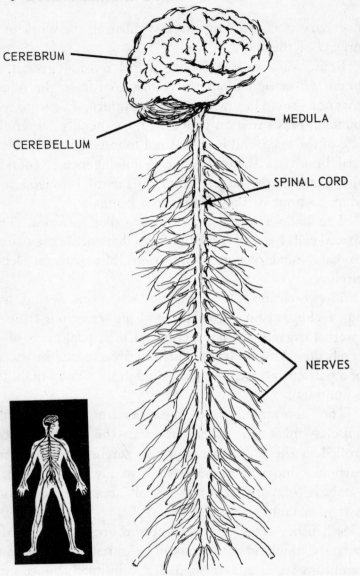

CEREBRUM

MEDULA

CEREBELLUM

SPINAL CORD

NERVES

The central nervous system

Computers can perform marvels in "memorizing" data and in solving problems from these data, much faster and more accurately than a man can do. But it was a brain that invented the computer.

Have you ever tried to walk a straight line, or to walk along a narrow stone fence? Have you ever seen a tight-rope performer in the circus walk, run, or ride a bicycle across tightly stretched wire? Many muscles of the back, legs, and even the arms are used in balancing oneself for each of these stunts. Even stitting or standing erect requires the interaction of many muscles. Coordinating and controlling them to produce a balance is the work of the cerebellum. It is done automatically.

If you had to think to keep your heart beating, your respiratory muscles working, and the muscles of your alimentary canal pushing food along, you would not have time for much else. These vital activities must continue without pause; any stoppage would be fatal. They are automatically controlled in the medulla of the brain. This is the brain's smallest part, but by no means the least important one. Here, too, coughing, sneezing, swallowing, blinking, and the production of digestive juices are controlled.

Nerves are the lines of communication between the brain and the organs of the body. They carry nerve impulses from one to the other. The movement of a nerve impulse may be compared with that of an electric current in a copper wire; and, actually, the speed with which both move is about the same.

Nerves that carry impulses from sense organs are called

sensory; those that carry command impulses to muscles are called motor. A third kind, called secretory, carries impulses to glands, which, as a result, make their juices.

Sensory and motor nerves are independent of one another. If a sensory nerve is touched, it results in a sensation; if a motor nerve is touched, it results in a movement, the contraction of a muscle. For example, one may get a cut on the palm of the hand; immediately one of the fingers feels numb, although it can still be moved. Though the sensory nerve from it has been cut, the motor nerve is intact.

As you learned earlier, the nerves that enter and leave the brain (except those of the head) do so through the spinal cord. This cable of nerves gives off branches to the arms, legs, and organs of the body, and it receives sensory nerves from sense organs (except those of the head.)

Voluntary movements are controlled by the motor areas in the cerebrum. However, the control is often delegated to other control centers, with the result that the response is quicker and the brain (the cerebrum) is relieved of the responsibility. For example, if you should touch a hot object, you would pull your hand away instantly—before you could feel the sensation of heat. The sensory impulse would have been passed to the spinal cord, which acts as a nerve center. The spinal cord would have sent out a motor impulse to the muscles of the arm, causing your hand to be instantly withdrawn. In the meantime, the sensory impulse would have passed on to the brain, making you aware of the heat.

Such control of voluntary muscular movements by centers other than the cerebrum, or even by the cerebrum when it is done without conscious awareness, is called reflex control. The movements that are controlled in the medulla are, of course, reflex.

Many movements controlled by the cerebrum may become reflex. You become more efficient as a result. Can you remember learning to write, carefully tracing each letter? Do you remember learning to knit, to swim, to typewrite, or to play a musical instrument? When you start to learn any of these skills you must "keep your mind on what you are doing." You must work consciously. As you repeat the act again and again you do so with less and less attention to it, until it becomes automatic. It has become a habit, a learned reflex act.

What we believe happens is this: The sensory nerve path and the motor nerve path for the act become so well established that the connection between the two is made instantly, without thought. This is "natural automation."

To make an act a habit it must be practiced frequently and regularly with a will; you must *want* to do it. This explains why so many children who are given music lessons do not learn to play well. Practice for them is a bore and a chore; they do it reluctantly. You must practice an act the correct way each time, giving it your full attention. Then you must repeat the act correctly until it becomes automatic. "Correct practice makes perfect."

It is fortunate that so many of your everyday, routine activities can be made habits. Otherwise, you would have to pay attention to so many trivial acts that there would be little time and energy to learn more interesting and important ones. If, in writing, you had to think how to form each letter, you could not think of what it was that you wanted to write! Make a list of all your activities during a day. How many are habits, acts that you learned to do automatically? The length of the list will surprise you.

Bad habits can be formed as well as good ones, and can be "unlearned" only if you have a strong desire to do so. A bad habit must be made a conscious act again; you must be made aware that you are about to do it. Suppose a youngster has formed the habit of biting his fingernails. They look ugly, and they may even become infected and be painful. If he decides to give up the habit, how does he go about doing so? One solution might be to paint his fingernails with an unpleasant-tasting substance. Then, each time he brought one near his mouth, he would be reminded of what he was about to do. Such a reminder, coupled with a strong will and persistence, should enable him to give up the bad habit.

Sometimes a good habit may be substituted for a bad one. For example, the children of a certain neighborhood had a bad habit of daubing the store windows, fences, and doorways with paint on Halloween night "just for fun." The storekeepers thought of having a window painting contest for them. Paint and brushes were provided and prizes were given for the most interesting and most original paintings. It became an important community art project. The children took pride in it, and a bad habit was replaced by a good one.

Habit formation is not the only way of training one to behave in desirable ways at home and in school. Suppose mother wants Johnny to pick up his toys after play and put them in the toy box. She will say, "Please pick up your toys." With some persuasion, he will do so. She will say, "Thank you, Johnny. You are a good boy." Then she will reward him with a favorite cookie, or a coin for his bank. She will do it in the same way, day after day. Johnny will respond because he likes the praise and the cookie or coin. After a while he will make the right response even if the reward is omitted. This was one of the conditions for his doing the act. Now he responds without this condition. He does so automatically. Such a response is called a conditioned reflex. Like a habit, it is a *learned* reflex.

Conditioning must not be confused with bribery. Some youngsters—and grownups, too—will obey a request only if they are given something, or bribed. Some youngsters will throw a tantrum if they do not get something that they want. Bribing or giving in to a tantrum is not good conditioning.

Your central nervous system is comprised of the brain and its nerves; the sense organs; and the spinal cord and nerve fibers that extend from and to it.

There is another, the autonomic nervous system, that has a large role in controlling and coordinating the work of the vital organs. It is made up of a chain of clusters of nerve cells. Three of these clusters, especially large, are called plexuses. This entire chain is found near the spinal cord. The clusters are connected to one another and to the spinal cord by nerve fibers. Other nerve fibers extend from the clusters to the vital organs.

We may think of the autonomic nervous system as providing constant, automatic supervision of the vital organs. The central nervous system is thereby relieved of this function. But the central and the autonomic nervous systems are interdependent. For example, the beating of the heart is controlled by nerve fibers from both systems. And any disorder in a vital organ is made known in the brain by means of pain signals.

Another kind of control and regulation is supplied by chemical "messengers" called hormones. These are produced in certain glands that are live chemical factories. The hormones pass directly from the glands into the blood stream and are carried about to the organs whose work they control or regulate.

For example, the thyroid glands, found on either side of the throat near the larynx, produce the hormone thyroxin. This hormone regulates the rate of energy production in the body. Too little thyroxin in the blood slows up the body activity so much that a person behaves in a listless and sluggish manner. An excess of the hormone in the blood makes one overactive. To make thyroxin, the thyroid gland needs iodine, a mineral that must be supplied in food or drinking water.

The pancreas, you will recall, is an important digestive gland. It is also an important hormone gland. Within it, there are many patches of cells that manufacture the hormone insulin. This hormone regulates the use and storage of sugar in the body. A small amount of this nutrient circulates in the blood at all times to supply fuel to the cells. An excess of sugar in the blood is harmful to the cells. Insulin insures an adequate supply and controls the storage or excretion of the excess.

Failure of the pancreas to produce insulin results in a disease known as diabetes. A person who suffers from diabetes cannot utilize his sugar supply properly. The disease can be treated successfully by injections of insulin into the body, or by doses of insulin taken by mouth.

Just above the kidneys are the adrenal glands. They produce a number of important hormones. One of them, adrenin, helps you through emergencies, or "tough spots." Suppose you have to perform before an audience; make the win-or-lose play for your team; walk the last long mile on a scout hike. You may feel weak in the knees and have "butterflies in your stomach"; your teeth may chatter; you may get into a sweat. Then you get a grip on yourself, and not only do the job, but do it well!

You are able to meet these emergencies because adrenin has circulated in the blood. It causes sugar to be released from the liver into the blood stream for the cells; the heart beats faster and more firmly; the arteries contract, raising the blood pressure; breathing becomes deeper. The body is keyed up for the emergency. Great feats of valor, of strength, and of endurance have been performed "on the adrenals," under the influence of adrenin.

Hormones control and regulate these and other body functions: the growth of bones; the production of red corpuscles; the contraction of certain muscles; the balance of water in the cells and tissues; the changes in the body as one grows from girlhood and boyhood into young womanhood and young manhood.

The hormone glands do not work independently of one another but are coordinated into a system. The "master gland" appears to be the pituitary gland, found on the lower side of the brain. For example, the pituitary gland produces a hormone called ACTH, for short. This hormone stimulates the adrenal gland to produce the hormone cortisone, that doctors have found very helpful in treating many body disorders. Another pituitary hormone stimulates the adrenal gland to produce still another hormone that stimulates the production of red corpuscles in the marrow of bones.

The need for coordinating the work of the hormone glands must have occurred to you when you read about the opposite effects of insulin and adrenin. The effect of insulin is to get excess sugar *out* of the blood and stored, whereas the effect of adrenin is to put sugar *into* the blood from storage. Which one takes place at a given time depends on the needs of the body at that moment. Such needs can be determined by the sense organs and communicated to the hormone-control center from the central nervous system. Control of the body activities is, indeed, a team job.

To sum up, your vital activities are controlled unconsciously, without awareness on your part, by your autonomic nervous system, your hormone system, and to some extent by your central nervous system. Your routine activities are also unconsciously controlled—as habits, or conditioned reflexes—by the central nervous system. Thus, your mind is freed for conscious activity—to think, reason, plan, design, explore, experiment, discover, invent, appreciate. These are the activities that make up intelligent behavior.

:nine:
Developing sexual maturity

So far, this book has discussed the organ systems (and their functions) which are concerned with your everyday activities and with your adjustment to your environment. The reproductive system, the last one to mature, is concerned not only with the present but with the next generation.

As girls and boys approach the end of their pre-teen years, they become aware of great changes in the structure and form of their bodies, in their thinking and feeling, and in the functioning of their reproductive organs. The changes often start a year or two earlier in girls than in boys. In short, sometime between the ages of eleven and fourteen years, girls and boys enter the period of puberty. This is the beginning of adolescence.

Among many peoples, both civilized and primitive, puberty is regarded as the "coming of age" of girls and of boys. The event is celebrated with religious ceremonies and social festivities. In primitive societies the girls are immediately accepted into the company of women, the boys into the company of men. In civilized societies, where the cultural and economic demands on young people are much greater, the girls and boys usually remain dependent upon their parents through adolescence, and often beyond it. During this time, they receive the education and training that will enable them to become independent of their parents, and to take their places in the community as responsible adults.

When girls reach puberty, their ovaries start functioning, so that one (usually) ovum, egg cell, ripens every twenty-eight days (although this schedule may vary by a few days, and even skip a month occasionally). Ova will thus be produced for about thirty years, interrupted only during periods of pregnancy. At puberty, the testes of boys begin to function. They will produce sperm cells, without a schedule, almost to the end of life. Ova and sperm cells are reproductive cells; they may produce a new generation.

Also beginning at puberty, the ovaries produce a hormone which stimulates the development of the feminine characteristics that distinguish a young lady from a young girl. The body becomes more shapely, the face becomes more mature, hair grows on parts of the body and the breasts enlarge. Similarly, the testes produce a hormone that stimulates the development of those masculine characteristics that make young men of young boys. Their bodies become more broad-shouldered and more muscular, hair grows on the face and other parts of the body, and the voice deepens as the vocal cords become longer.

At puberty, the entire body experiences a considerable growth spurt. This begins a year or two earlier in girls than in boys. Both pass through an "awkward age" (although not at the same time), during which they appear gangling because their limbs get a head start in growth over their trunks. They are sensitive about their appearances until the growth of the trunk catches up to that of the limbs. Because they develop a little earlier, in early adolescence girls lose interest in boys of their age group and show a greater interest in older boys. However, friendly relations are restored as the boys catch up in growth and development.

There are significant changes in the way girls and boys think and feel as they enter into and pass through their teen years. At first most of them become more serious about their school work and they show more interest in school activities. Later they become interested in and concerned about conditions in their environment. More and more they think about and plan their futures. This is mentally healthy provided the thinking is done realistically in terms of one's abilities, and with such competent advice and guidance as one may be able to get.

As they progress through the teens, adolescents become more and more insistent on having more independence. This is normal and mentally healthy. This problem is discussed in Chapter 10. Wise parents understand when and how to relinquish parental authority, as the adolescent shows increasing capacity for making his own decisions and assuming responsibility for them. In this way, parents help adolescents to develop mental and emotional maturity.

Prior to puberty, most girls and boys do not show great interest in friendships with the opposite sex. As they enter adolescence they discover one another. Such interest and relationships are normal. If the young people have thought about and understood this book, and if they have assimilated the values and ideals taught by their families and their faiths, then wholesome boy-girl relationships will be preparation for mature love. It is physically and emotionally healthy to look forward to having children one day, and to want to pass on to those children the love and devotion one has received, or perhaps only wanted.

A new life begins when a mature, ripe egg cell unites with a sperm cell in the mother. This is called fertilization, and the result is a fertilized egg. It enters the uterus, where it becomes attached to the wall. This wall has undergone changes in preparing to receive the egg. Here, nourished by the blood of the mother, the fertilized egg develops.

Development consists, at first, in the multiplication of the fertilized egg. It divides in two; then each half divides in two. This process of cell multiplication continues until many trillion cells are formed.

Early in this period some cells become different from other cells. Groups of cells of the same kind form tissues, which, in turn, become organized to form organs.

The fertilized egg is microscopic in size. By the end of the third week it will have grown to the size of a grain of rice, about one quarter of an inch. It is called an embryo, an undeveloped, immature living thing. It bears no resemblance to the baby that it will become.

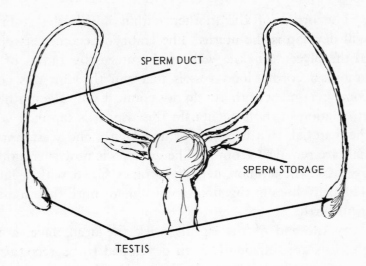

Male reproductive organs

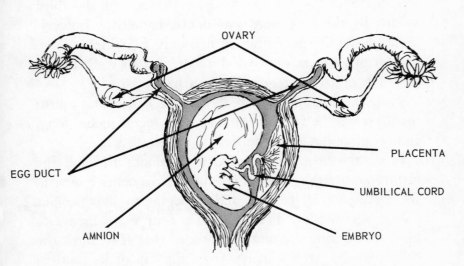

Female reproductive organs in early pregnancy

The organ of the mother within which the embryo will develop is the uterus. The embryo becomes attached to the placenta in the wall of the uterus by means of an umbilical cord. Blood vessels that run through this cord come in contact with but do not connect with the mother's circulation in the placenta. In this way it is supplied with the materials that it needs for its growth, and waste materials are removed from it. The embryo is now surrounded by a sac, the amnion, which becomes fiilled with a fluid. The baby lives in this fluid environment until the moment of its birth.

By the end of the eighth week the head, face, arms, and legs are sufficiently well developed to be recognized for what they will become. Yet the embryo is only one inch in length.

It becomes known as a fetus at the end of the third month. By this time there is no doubt that a baby is developing in the uterus. Although it is only four inches long, and weighs a mere ounce and a half, it is so well formed that it is clearly recognizable as a baby.

Now the fetus grows rapidly. At the end of the fourth month it will be from six and a half to eight inches long, and weigh about seven ounces.

From the beginning of the fifth month through the eighth month, the fetus grows about two inches a month. Its organs are all formed and it begins to move about within the mother. The fetus adds four more inches to its stature during the ninth month, so that at its birth the baby may be twenty inches from the top of its head to its heels. It will weigh, on the average, between six and eight pounds.

The time has come for the fetus to leave the security, warmth, and dependence that it has had within the mother. It emerges through the birth canal, with the assistance of a doctor. The miracle of the birth of a baby, a new life, takes place.

A newborn babe is quite helpless. Although it has been separated from its mother by the cutting of the umbilical cord, it remains dependent upon her, and now upon the father too, for food, shelter, clothing, and the training and education that it will need first to survive, then to find a place in the world into which it was born. And from the first it will need understanding and love to grow health-fully.

Most families in this country have only two or three children; some have as many as ten or more. But a woman produces as many as four hundred mature eggs during her fertile period of about thirty years. What becomes of those that are not fertilized, that are not developed into babies?

Every twenty-eight days or so the ovaries discharge a mature ovum into an egg tube through which it passes to the uterus. At the same time, the tissues of the wall of the uterus prepare to receive a fertilized egg. If there are no sperm cells in the egg tube, so that the egg is not fertilized, the specially prepared tissues of the wall of the uterus are discarded. Together with the unfertilized egg and some blood, they are discharged from the body. This is men-struation.

The periodic cycle that includes ovulation (the release of a mature ovum) and the "monthly" menstrual discharge is controlled by a hormone from the pituitary gland which acts like a time clock for the purpose. Menstruation is interrupted normally during pregnancy and may be interrupted occasionally, briefly, for other reasons. The loss of blood is normal and should not be alarming. If, however, it is excessive, and is accompanied by uncomfortable cramping pains, a doctor should be consulted.

Boys and men have no comparable discharge since the production of sperm cells is not periodic. In early adolescence boys may have occasional emissions of semen during the night. Semen is a fluid containing sperm cells. Such emissions soon stop as the newly functioning reproductive system becomes controlled.

Sexual maturity as a physiological function is attained when the organs of reproduction begin to function. Sexual maturity as a psychological function is achieved when a girl or a boy has developed an understanding and appreciation of the role of sex in the formation of a healthy personality.

:ten:

A healthy mind in a healthy body

You are well aware that you are growing up. You are reminded of it as you quickly grow out of your clothes and your shoes. You hear it from your relatives and friends —"My, how you have grown!" And you know it from the rule on the wall (or whatever way you have of measuring your height), and from the weight scale.

As your body frame, your skeleton, grows larger, your organs naturally do so also. Your growth is continuous, although not uniform, until you attain physical maturity— at about eighteen years of age for girls, about twenty-one years for boys. There are several spurts in your growth pattern, periods during which growth takes place more rapidly. There is one such spurt at about the age of twelve years. At this time girls pass boys of the same age in growth and development. The latter catch up a few years later.

As this spurt gets under way, many girls and boys suffer mental anxieties. The girls fear that they may grow too tall to be graceful and attractive. Boys, on the other hand, fear that they may not grow tall and robust enough to be impressive and attractive.

Your stature, as well as other body characteristics, are inherited. That is, they are passed on to you by your parents, grandparents, and even more distant ancestors. If you grow normally and healthfully, you will attain the stature that was already set for you at birth. If you want to grow tall you should have chosen tall parents, and even then you could not have been sure. A good mixed and balanced diet might add a few inches to one's height.

Girls and boys overcome these growth anxieties as they find acceptance in their families and among their friends, and as they learn that stature is not critical in achieving desired goals.

Still another growth problem causes mental distress among early teenage girls and boys. It results from the fact that the trunk and limbs do not grow at the same rate. The youngsters appear gangling and gawky, so that they feel ill at ease. This problem is discussed on page 117. By their mid-teens the growth problems are resolved, as girls and boys become well-formed young women and young men.

At the same time that the organs of the body are growing in size, the mind is expanding in depth. Your early years are, largely, a training period during which you learn, mainly through habit formation and conditioning, such everyday, necessary, routine behavior as walking, dressing, daily hygiene, table manners, reading, writing, and so on through the long list that you may complete. But even young children can think and reason and solve simple problems. Wise parents help them to do so by getting them educational toys, by encouraging them to express their opinions and to make suggestions. As they acquire more knowledge and experience, as their minds expand through use, children are able to think and reason more effectively, to solve more difficult problems.

You now know that the cerebrum is the receiving center for sensations that originate as stimuli in the sense organs. The neurons of the cerebrum receive and record the sensations, although we do not know how they do so. Such stored information becomes your memories. You may think of them as files of still and moving pictures; a library of sound and sight recordings; a collection of tastes, odors, and feelings.

The stored information, your memories, enable you to understand and appreciate new situations and experiences, and to solve new problems. The neurons in certain areas of the cerebrum are so interconnected that you can call upon their stored information for thinking, reasoning, inventing, problem solving, judging, and appreciating.

As young children are shown picture books, as they are told and read stories, as they are taken places, and as their many questions are patiently answered, their store of information grows, and their minds expand. Now, at your age, you are expected to learn more and more on your own, much of it through study. It is important, therefore, that you form good study habits early. Many girls and boys who do not do so, yet manage to "get by" in their early school years, find themselves in difficulty later on in high school or college when the going gets harder. With some mental distress and considerable effort they may learn to study; or they may become drop-outs.

To form good study habits, these rules must be practiced regularly, frequently, in the same way, and with a strong desire to follow them: (1) Set aside a definite time for study each day, when you are not likely to be interrupted by friends, fatigue, or hunger. (2) You should have a quiet place for study. If you try to listen to a radio or to a recording, or to watch a television program at the same time, you will not form effective study habits. (3) You should sit up straight in a comfortable but not too relaxing a chair. (4) Prepare all the material that you will need so that you will not interrupt yourself to get paper, pencil, or book. (5) Use a good light on your book or paper so that eye strain will not cause fatigue. (6) When you have completed your studying, test yourself to see how well you have accomplished what you had planned.

As you grow and your mind develops you want more and more responsibility for solving your own problems and for making your own decisions. It is mentally healthy that you should do these things, and that you should know how to do them. You must first have a very clear understanding of your problem. Then you should get together all the information about it that you can—from your own knowledge and experience, from books, from people who know about it, from experiments that you may perform. Next, you should study all the data until you find an answer that appears to be the best solution to your problem. You will have used your mind in working it out.

Further evidence of your mental growth is your demand for more and more independence. This is both natural and desirable. You must gradually learn to fend for yourself; to grow beyond the discipline of your parents toward self-discipline. The realization that their little girl or little boy has grown up comes as a shock to many parents, but they soon recognize their responsibility for helping their children grow toward maturity and independence. They will gradually relinquish their controls as you show your capability to assume the additional responsibilities.

On the other hand, you know that you are not demanding complete independence. There are such matters as food, shelter, clothing, and allowance that you are not ready to take over. Yours is a difficult growth period; no longer a child, not yet a young woman or young man. But with the understanding, encouragement, security, and love of your family you will successfully work out your problems of growing up.

At your age you want to be "like the other girls" or "like the other boys." This is quite natural. But you should think seriously about which girls or boys you want to be like. The choice of the right friends and companions will help you grow toward those desirable goals that you have set for yourself. The wrong choices can hold you back or pull you down.

Girls and boys usually have heroines or heroes—people they particularly admire and whom they would like to emulate. You may have found such persons in television, in sports, in your reading, among your teachers, older relatives, and friends. You should ask yourself, "What is there about my heroine (or hero) that I particularly admire? Is this trait or accomplishment truly admirable?" Here, too, the proper choice will help you grow to be the kind of young woman or young man you want to be. The wrong choice may put you off your course.

Of the girls and boys that you know, how many do you rate as friends (not just classmates or acquaintances)? Sharing adventures with friends makes them more interesting; sharing thoughts makes them more understandable; sharing problems helps to solve them.

Some girls and boys find it difficult to make friends. They are shy—lack confidence in themselves. This is called a feeling of insecurity. Such a feeling may be the result of their not being given opportunities to speak up, make suggestions, take part in family discussions. "Little children should be seen and not heard" is not good training for later social living.

Some shy girls and boys try to attract attention to themselves as a means of feeling important, acquiring status. A girl may do so by letting her fingernails grow very long; a boy may do so by letting his hair grow long and unruly. But such behavior will not win them the recognition and the friends that they crave. They should seek such satisfactions in worthwhile activities—excellence in school work; participation in school activities; earning merit badges in Boy or Girl Scout organizations; developing a worthwhile interest or hobby that will make them more interesting girls and boys now, more interesting young women and young men later. These are mentally healthy ways of overcoming feelings of insecurity and inadequacy. They contribute to the development of a healthy personality.

Think of an adult that you know who has impressed you very favorably. He or she will undoubtedly have qualities such as these: is clean and well-groomed, dresses neatly and in good taste, has a pleasant voice, is friendly and understanding, has a sense of humor and smiles easily, is tolerant, has many interests. In short, he or she has a good personality.

On the other hand, you may know someone who is slovenly in person and dress, has an unpleasant voice, is generally out of sorts, inclined to criticize and scold. Such traits characterize a poor personality.

Personality is described by the qualities that one shows in one's behavior toward others. The outward traits reflect the physical, mental, and emotional well-being of the body. Thus a person in pain is not likely to be pleasant or in a good humor. A person with strong prejudices is not likely to be understanding. And one who lives in fear is not likely to be outgoing. A good, healthy personality is the product of a healthy mind in a healthy body.

A child may be born with a physical disability. A person may acquire a disability as a result of an accident or of disease. The handicap may well affect the mental and emotional activity of the child or grown up. With proper treatment and care the handicapped person may learn to function healthfully in all respects, within his limitations. The late President Franklin Delano Roosevelt suffered from poliomyelitis as an adult. As a result he became paralyzed in both legs. Yet he subsequently served as President of these United States for three full terms during a very critical period in our history. Helen Keller, one of the most honored women of our time, has lived a long and useful life, yet she has been unable to see or hear, and scarcely to talk. Do you know a handicapped girl or boy who is doing a good job, with a pleasant and cheerful disposition?

Emotions are strong, natural feelings such as gladness, sadness, joy, sorrow, fear, rage, hate, love. Very young children are not able to control their emotions as well as you or adults can. You know this from the cries of babies and from the tantrums of little girls and little boys. As you grow up and improve in your ability to think and reason, you learn to control your emotions. You never do control them altogether, nor should you, for there are times when you feel very deeply about persons, events, things. But when girls and boys, or even adults, throw tantrums, it is evidence of emotional immaturity; they have not grown up emotionally.

The body, the mind, and the personality are inseparable

The emotional state is reflected in the facial expression

parts of one person. Each affects the work of the others, and is in turn affected by them. If one suffers even so mild an ailment as indigestion, he will not think clearly, and he will very likely be irritable and unfriendly. On the other hand, if one eats while mentally disturbed or angry, he may well suffer indigestion. A person who is quite ill physically may be given occupational therapy, something to do that will keep his mind active and his spirits somewhat more hopeful. It helps recovery.

The brain is not the mind, although the mind is housed in the brain. Nor is the mind an organ, so it cannot be studied as the other organs have been. However, despite great difficulties, the mind is being studied, to learn how it works and how one behaves when one is mentally healthy; to discover what goes wrong when one becomes mentally ill; to find means of restoring the mentally ill to mental health.

The study of the mind is called psychology. Psychologists use tests and direct observation to discover what is normal, healthy thinking and behavior; and what is abnormal, unhealthy thinking and behavior.

The recognition that the mind may become sick, and that it may often be restored to health is still a recent development in medical practice. Most people will talk freely about their physical ills and operations, past and present, but they remain silent about any mental illness that they may have had, or have.

Many children are born with impaired minds that are incapable of normal development. The impairment may be the result of an unfortunate abnormal development before birth, or it may result from brain damage during birth. Such children may be mentally retarded, capable of only slow and limited mental growth. Some may be mentally deficient, severely retarded.

In the past, most people's attitudes toward the mentally ill or retarded lacked understanding and sympathy. The mentally ill were considered "queer," "lunatics," or "crazy." Mentally retarded children were "dunces" or "dopes." Regrettably, such attitudes may still be found. Mental illness and mental retardation are misfortunes, not disgraces.

Mental illness is extremely widespread. In most instances the mentally ill person is able to do his work and to get along in his social life, but sometimes with tension and often unhappily. A seriously mentally ill person cannot carry on his normal activities effectively, if at all; he may withdraw from the company of people, or may become so aggressive as to be a menace to them. People sometimes use the term "nervous breakdown" to describe severe mental illness.

The causes of mental illness are not known, except in a general way. The minds of some people are less able than others to stand the stresses and strains that may beset one—overwork, a sudden shock, a lack or loss of security, for example. The breakdown may come long after the original cause occurred. It may lie deeply buried in the mind.

The treatment of mental diseases has made great progress in the past fifty years. Psychiatrists and psychoanalysts, doctors who specialize in the treatment of these diseases, use somewhat different methods to get the same result—

the restoration of the patient to mental health. Mental hospitals that are planned and organized to treat the mentally ill are a far cry from the old "asylums" where the sick were confined as inmates rather than treated as patients.

What do girls and boys need to grow up to be healthy young women and young men? It was once believed, and you may have thought, from your reading of the earlier chapters of this book, that satisfying the basic physical needs would do the job. These needs include a good diet, fresh air, adequate clothing and shelter, sufficient exercise and rest, and protection from infectious disease. But what of a healthy mental development? The means of promoting it do not come from any material things. From infancy to maturity, girls and boys, must be supplied with generous amounts of understanding, encouragement, security, appreciation, and love. Then they will develop into whole persons, healthy in mind and in personality as well as in body.

:eleven:

Safeguarding your food, water, and air

The food stores in which your grandmothers and great-grandmothers marketed were far different from our modern food supermarkets. At that time, foods were sold from "bulk" containers. Crackers were taken by the handful from large boxes; sugar and flour were scooped from barrels; cereals came from bags and bins; and milk was dipped from large cans. All foods were exposed to dust and germs, flies and insects, and sometimes to handling by customers —from the bread, rolls, and cakes in the bake shop to the uncovered cuts of meat in the butcher shop. Refrigeration, as we know it, was unheard of, and inadequate ice boxes often contaminated the food they were supposed to preserve.

This should make us appreciate the modern packaging of foods in sealed containers or paper cartons, or in plastic

A grocery store of yesterday

wrap or aluminum foil. Such packaging is usually done automatically by clean machinery in dust-free and germ-free plants, many of which are air-conditioned.

FOOD

The marketing of milk offers a good illustration of how a basic food is safeguarded from production to consumption. Milk spoils rapidly, and was once a prime cause of

A modern supermarket

spreading strep sore throat, typhoid fever, dysentery, and food poisoning. Today, this essential food is processed in accordance with the strictest government standards. Cows are now inspected for possible diseases, and the law requires that they be housed in clean barns, that their udders be washed before milking, and that milking equipment be sterilized. Dairy workers must also be disease-free.

The milk is kept at a specified temperature (usually 50° Fahrenheit) prior to delivery to the processing plant. There it is pasteurized, by being heated for thirty minutes between 140° to 145°; or by being heated to 160° for

Processing milk: pasteurization/homogenization

These storage tanks for pasteurized milk are cooled by ther-
mostatically-controlled ice water within their stainless steel
walls

fifteen seconds as a flowing stream of milk. Though pas-
teurizing does not destroy all the germs in milk, it kills
those that may cause disease.

The milk is then automatically bottled and sealed in
sterile bottles or cartons, and again cooled to 50°. It should
be delivered in refrigerated trucks to the stores, kept
refrigerated until sold, and be refrigerated in the home until
it is used. Then you can drink it, confident of its purity.

Your food supply is also safeguarded, as well as greatly
enriched, by modern methods of freezing. Vegetables are
picked and packed at the peak of ripeness and freshness and

are quick-frozen. Fish, poultry, and many other foods that are frozen are safe, wholesome, and nutritious, since this method preserves their vitamin content.

Modern canning of fruits, vegetables, fish, and meats by vacuum sealing—heating under pressure and sealing automatically—not only prevents spoilage but also preserves the nutrients in the foods. Other foods are preserved by dehydration (drying), smoking, and salting; or, chemicals may be added as preservatives. Such chemicals must be approved as safe for health by the Pure Food and Drug Administration.

When you buy meats, you may rest assured that the animals have been inspected for freedom from diseases,

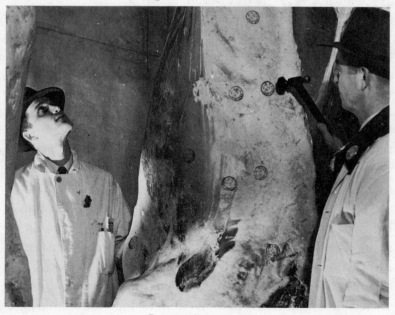

Inspecting meat

that the meats have been graded for quality, and that they are being sold under conditions regulated by the federal, state, and local health departments. These require standard sanitary conditions in the store; sanitary display of meats; proper refrigeration.

Many communities require that all food handlers— butchers, bakers, cooks, waiters, and others—obtain a food handler's health certificate. These workers are examined regularly by the department of health to make sure they have no disease that they may transmit while handling food.

Protecting your food supply is a team job that enlists the cooperation of food producers; food processors; food distributors; food merchants; federal, state, and local departments of health and of agriculture; and, finally, the cooperation of the consumers—you and your family.

WATER

Water is the most abundant substance on Earth, and the complete story of its many uses would fill a large book. We are interested in it here only as a nutrient, as an aid in preparing food, and as a body and household cleanser.

Despite its great abundance, water is not free, especially for people living in towns and cities. It costs a great deal of money to deliver a safe, wholesome supply, often brought from a considerable distance. A watershed, a great tract of land containing a natural water system, must be acquired. The rivers and lakes of the watershed will become the water supply of the town or the city. Huge dams must be built to form great reservoirs, like large lakes, in which the water is stored. There it must be made free of objectionable tastes and odors, as well as free of germs that may cause disease. Finally, the water must be delivered to the homes of the people in the area. All this is paid for from taxes.

Rain water, while free of germs, is tasteless. This is because it lacks the minerals that are found in water that has passed over or through the soil. Minerals not only flavor water, but they promote good health.

For instance, iodine in very minute quantities is needed by the body to make thyroxin, a chemical that helps to regulate respiration. The water in some regions lacks iodine, as do the foods commonly used. As a result of the lack of iodine, many people suffer from an enlargement of the thyroid gland and of the neck, a condition known as goiter. In such regions, iodine is often added to the drinking water.

Fluorides are minerals that are found naturally in some waters, but are lacking in others. A minute amount of these minerals makes the enamel covering of the teeth, especially those of young children, very hard and resistant to decay. Doctors and dentists have found that young people up to the age of fourteen who drink water containing sufficient fluorides have 60 percent fewer cavities than do those who drink water lacking these minerals. Tooth decay is second only to common colds as the principal health problem of girls and boys. Adding enough fluorides to make one part in a million parts of water gives the desired protection.

Residents of smaller communities may get their water

Chemical wastes from this wood pulp factory pollute the stream, while the chimneys belch pollutants into the air

from deep wells. This water is usually safe, for chances are it has been filtered, or strained, through a deep layer of soil and sand.

Cities use surface water that has run off from the soil into streams, ponds, and lakes. These sources are very likely to become polluted—a major health problem in many areas of our country today.

How do the waters become polluted? Factories dump their chemical wastes into streams, so that the water is no longer drinkable. Towns and cities pour their sewage into them so that the water is no longer free from germs that cause disease. The germs of water-borne diseases come from the intestinal wastes of sick people, or from those who carry such germs even though they themselves may

Aerating water

not be sick. These diseases include typhoid fever, diarrhea, and dysentery.

Water may to a large extent purify itself of the plant and animal refuse in it. "Good" bacteria in the water and in the soil feed upon and destroy the refuse, changing it into materials that plants can use for their growth. While water is stored in a reservoir, these bacteria work upon the refuse.

To remove the floating particles that make water muddy, it is filtered through a bed of sand in the reservoir. The water may also be cleared with a chemical, such as alum, that swells to form a sticky mass in which the particles in the water are caught. This mass sinks to the bottom of the reservoir, from which it is removed.

Harmful germs in the water are destroyed by fresh air and sunlight, or chlorine gas, or both. When you visit a reservoir you may see water being sprayed high into the air. This is not a fountain display. Exposure to oxygen in the air and to sunlight will kill many of the bacteria in the water.

Many communities chlorinate their water for safety.

Chlorinating water

Three to five pounds of chlorine gas are used to one million gallons of water for purification. The chlorine kills bacteria and other tiny plants that grow in the water.

Safeguarding the water supply is a cooperative job of the state and local governments. A stream often flows through several counties, a lake may border on many. Hence statewide regulations are needed to prevent water pollution. However, insuring the safety of the water supply of a community is primarily the responsibility of the local government. The responsibility is shared by the state water and health departments.

There are times when you yourself may need to know how to make your own safe water supply—when you are on a hike or picnic, for example. If you should stop at a public campsite or picnic ground you would very likely find a safe supply, under the supervision of the state or county board of health. You would be told of its safety by a sign.

But you may have occasion to stop, or even pitch a tent, beside a brook or a spring out in the wilds. If you want insurance against infection from germs in the water, boil it and then cool it before using. You can also get chlorine tablets, before going camping, to kill the germs, though the tablets will probably give the water an unpleasant taste.

On a camping trip, be sure also to use sterilized water to wash your teeth, your hands, any fruits or vegetables that are eaten raw or unpeeled, and any glasses and dishes that you use. After going to all this trouble, you will appreciate the safe water supply that you have at home.

AIR

Having read about the respiratory system, you already know that a supply of fresh air is essential for the production of energy by the cells. How good is the air that you breathe?

The habitable atmosphere in which we live is a vast ocean of air. We live at the bottom of it. Basically a mixture of gases, "pure" air is a little less than four-fifths nitrogen, one-fifth oxygen, and a minute fractional part composed of rather rare gases. "Pure" air, however, does not exist.

Even in regions of the earth where no people live the air becomes mixed with other gases and with tiny particles of solid material. Air is not still, but moves about as winds, picking up loose soil particles, and sometimes reaching the density of a sand storm. The decay of dead plants and animals adds solid particles and other gases to the air. Flowers shed showers of pollen, and fungous plants send torrents of spores into the air to be carried about by the winds, along with myriads of bacteria. All these contribute to making air the varied mixture that it is.

Air becomes polluted, or fouled, when it carries gases and solid particles that are unpleasant to smell and irritating to the respiratory tract, or when it carries disease-causing germs. Pollution is greatest over large cities. Riding in an airplane, high in the atmosphere, one can recognize the approach to a large city by the haze of polluted air that hangs over it. Many different sources contribute to building up such a haze.

The breathing of thousands of people living in crowded

cities sends a constant stream of carbon dioxide into the air. People add other pollutants, too. Smoke from cigarettes, cigars, and pipes adds considerable carbon dioxide and other gases, some of them poisonous in large quantities. It also adds soot. Uncovered coughs and sneezes spray tiny drops of saliva into the air, carrying bacteria with them. Dried saliva and phlegm, from spitting, add even more.

The furnaces that heat the homes and apartments of a city and that burn its refuse spew forth millions of pounds of pollutants each day. What you see pouring out of the chimneys are the solid particles, the soot. What you cannot see are the irritating, sometimes poisonous gases that come out of chimneys, too.

A furnace in good repair produces less pollution because it burns up fuel or refuse more completely. Moreover, some fuels produce more pollution than others, in this order: soft coal, hard coal, oil, and gas. Gas produces the least.

Most of the irritating, even poisonous, gas pollutants in the air over our cities come from the exhaust pipes of automobiles, motor trucks, and motor buses. They produce streams of dangerous fumes; one of the gases, carbon monoxide, has caused many deaths when people sat in closed cars with the motor running. A lesser, but still considerable, source of air pollution from motor vehicles results from the abrasion, or rubbing, of tires against concrete or asphalt roads. Very fine particles of rubber and of road material are added to the other pollutants in the air.

The ninety million passenger cars, motor trucks, and buses now on our roads and streets are a major health menace. Automobile engineers are studying how to design engines that will burn the fuel more completely with fewer waste products of gases and solid particles. They are also working on designs for an exhaust system that will destroy the air-polluting waste products. Automobiles driven by electric storage batteries produce no pollutants; but present models, still largely experimental, are limited in speed and in the distance they can travel without re-charging.

Most of the solid pollutants in the air come from the smoke that belches from factory smokestacks; from the burning of fuel; and from the dust that results from grind-ing, milling, and other manufacturing operations. Many of these solid pollutants can be trapped and kept out of the air. Indeed, Pittsburgh, once called the "Smoky City" because of the thick haze that hung over it, has almost completely cleared its atmosphere of such pollutants.

The gas pollutants, whether from factories, motor cars, or homes, are of two kinds: non-poisonous gases that are

The towering skyscraper buildings of Manhattan Island in the City of New York can scarcely be seen through the haze of the polluted air

merely a nuisance because of their disagreeable odors; and irritating and poisonous gases such as carbon monoxide, sulphur dioxide, nitrogen oxide, and a few others from some industries. Gases are much more difficult to keep out of the air.

Two other sources of air pollution have become menacing in recent years. The first comes from airplanes spraying crop plants and forest trees with poisons to kill insects. These poisons can be dangerous even when they fall on the plants for which they are intended. Some of them get into streams and lakes that become part of a water supply. Eaten (with plants) or drunk (in contaminated water), they are stored in a person's body, where they become a health hazard. And winds carry them about so that they may be breathed, as well.

Atomic energy—which can bring such great benefits— poses a most serious threat to the health of people all over the earth through air pollution. An atomic explosion in the air produces an immense dust cloud, whose particles become radioactive. Currents in the upper atmosphere carry these particles around the earth, keeping them aloft for many years, and letting them down gradually as "fallout." The radioactive particles pollute streams and lakes, food and water, and are taken into and stored in the body where they may be the cause of many ills.

Very heavily polluted air may become mixed with fog, haze, or dust. Thus, smoke and fog form smog; smoke and haze, smaze; smoke and dust, smust. After a while, each of these mixtures rises into the upper atmosphere.

In some regions, however, conditions in the atmosphere

The city of Denver, Colorado, under smog

are occasionally turned topsy-turvy. Instead of the warm air rising, it remains like a blanket of hot air over the smog and prevents it from escaping. The eyes of people living in the smog smart, respiratory organs are irritated, and respiratory diseases, as well as deaths from them, increase.

Sometimes the air over a large area becomes heavily polluted with germs. Then an epidemic of a respiratory disease such as influenza may occur. At such a time it is wise to avoid large crowds or close contact with people, as in crowded buses.

How can the pollution of air be lessened? It must be a total, cooperative effort that includes factory owners, householders, and all the public departments that can help —the departments of health, sanitation, buildings, and air pollution control. Neighboring communities, even states, must cooperate, since the pollutants are so readily carried about by winds.

The kinds, amounts, and sources of the air pollutants must be discovered. Means of trapping or destroying them before they get into the atmosphere must be studied. The air we breathe must not be allowed to become a dump for noxious, poisonous refuse.

The air that we breathe in the streets remains polluted, and the improvement of this air is recognized as a herculean job. However, the air that we breathe in homes, stores, offices, factories, and auditoriums can be, and has been, improved in an ever-increasing number of situations. It is done by air-conditioning.

Depending on their efficiency, air-conditioners filter dust, other solid pollutants, and some germs from the air. The humidity of the air is regulated for comfort as water vapor is removed from moist air, or added to dry air. The air is cooled or warmed according to the season. Moreover, the air is circulated, as a constant stream of fresh air is supplied and the used air drawn off.

The contrast between the inside and the outside air sharpens the demand for improvement of the polluted air of the street. Progress is being made, and you may look forward to breathing cleaner air in the streets.

:twelve:

Defending your body against disease

When you read about germs in food, germs in water, and germs in the air, does it amaze you that you manage to stay healthy most of the time? The reason you can is because your body has defenses, and you can get help in fighting off invading germs.

Who are your germ enemies? They are microorganisms, which means "very little living things." This includes bacteria, viruses, and a few one-celled animals. You may wonder how such tiny things can make girls and boys, woman and men, sick. It is because the invading germs find the environment in the body very favorable for their activity and development. They multiply in enormous numbers, so that they can be very damaging.

Bacteria are so small that microscopes with lenses of very high magnification are needed to see them. And even then, the germs, which are transparent, must be stained with color to be made visible.

There are three kinds of bacteria: those that are like tiny sticks, called bacilli; the even tinier ball-shaped ones, called cocci; and those that are twisted sticks, like one or more turns of a corkscrew, called spirilli.

Many bacteria are useful. They flavor ripened cheeses, for example. They also cause dead plants and animals to decay in the soil, producing the mineral salts that plants use for food. The plants, in turn, make the vegetables, fruits, and grains that we use for food. These bacteria also help to purify water by destroying sewage in it.

It is important to know which bacteria cause diseases; how they get into the body; and what damage they do. Some bacteria destroy tissues, as do the bacilli of tuberculosis; others produce poisons, as do the bacilli of diphtheria and tetanus (lockjaw).

Viruses are so very tiny that they can only be seen with the most powerful electron microscope, capable of magnifying 200,000 times (you read about this microscope earlier). In the body these viruses cause diseases such as the common cold and influenza by entering the cells and impairing their work.

The skin is a defense, a barrier against the invasion of the body by certain bacteria—so long as it remains unbroken. Bacteria are everywhere: on the skin, on the clothing, on an object that breaks through the skin. They are readily carried into any opening.

Moderate-sized, or even small cuts or scrapes should be treated with an antiseptic and covered with a sterile bandage. Invading germs will thus be killed, and others will be kept out. They will not get a foothold in the wound; there will be no infection; and the tissues will heal under the scab that is formed.

"Clean" cuts that bleed freely are not likely to become infected. The bacteria will be washed away by the flow of blood. Such wounds will usually be treated by a doctor, who will make sure that no germs invade the cut after his treatment.

If a wound is not well cared for, the area about it becomes red, swollen, warm, and painful. These are the signs of an inflammation; signs that the tissues have been invaded and are combating the invasion.

An abscess results when pus forms in the inflamed area. This is made up of some fluid from the blood or lymph, some red corpuscles, masses of white ones, and bacteria. The pus is held in a pocket that is formed as tissue is destroyed, and that becomes walled off from the surrounding normal tissue.

After a time the skin above the pocket of pus will break, and the pus will ooze out; or it may have to be lanced. In the escaping liquid are dead white corpuscles, dead bacteria, destroyed tissue. Other white corpuscles clean up the debris in the pocket after the infection has been conquered. Thus do the cells of the body contribute to its defense against the invasion of germs.

Some kinds of bacteria may invade the blood stream directly. This is "blood poisoning." The white corpuscles "eat" and destroy many of them, or are destroyed by them. Cells in the liver, the bone marrow, and the lymph nodes may also destroy the bacteria.

When your body needs help in repelling invading

germs, your doctors may rely on antibiotics. These drugs attack germs by interfering with the conditions the germs require in order to live. About a dozen antibiotic drugs are in common use. You may know of penicillin, aureomycin, streptomycin, and others.

The tissues of the body have a remarkable power to overcome germs or their poisonous products (toxins). The cells produce antibodies that fight against them, and if enough are produced quickly enough, the invasion may be overcome. A surplus of antibodies will be left in the blood to protect the body against a repeated infection by the same kinds of germs. This is called immunity—the power to resist disease. Each kind of antibody is effective against a specific kind of germ. This explains, for example, why a youngster who has recovered from measles will not suffer another attack.

If you are an average girl or boy, you have had at least five kinds of shots, each of which has given you immunity to a disease that once plagued young children. Shots aren't pleasant to take, but they may have spared you the suffering and sometimes crippling effects of smallpox, diphtheria, whooping cough, tetanus, and polio.

Most children are now protected against these diseases. Many of you have been, or perhaps someday will be, immunized against still others. Should your water supply become contaminated, you would be immunized against typhoid fever. A youngster bitten by a mad dog may be immunized against rabies.

With the scratch or jab of a sterile needle, the doctor injects into your tissues a vaccine or a serum. A vaccine contains the killed or weakened germs of a specific disease.

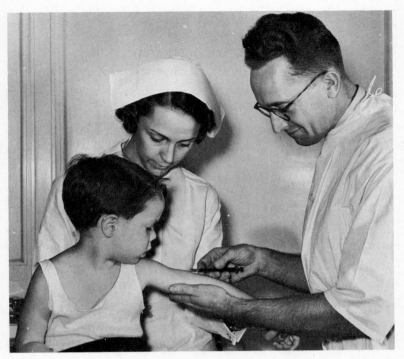

Smallpox can be prevented—by vaccination

Your tissues respond by producing bodies that can protect you against an invasion of live, virulent germs of that specific disease. A serum is a liquid made from the blood plasma of an animal (usually a horse) that has produced protective antibodies against the toxins or poisons of specific bacteria.

Smallpox was once a dreaded plague. Repeated epidemics of the disease killed hundreds of thousands of people throughout Europe. Those who recovered were "pockmarked"—that is, the skin of their faces was covered with small pits, left when the numerous scabs fell off. The disease spread to this country in colonial days. George Washington was one of its victims. Many people infected themselves from the sores of victims, in the hope that they might have a mild attack that would leave them immune to a more virulent one. Sometimes it worked; other times it did not.

Almost two hundred years ago, people in England knew that when milkmaids and men who worked in cow barns caught cowpox, they did not thereafter develop smallpox.

The animals had sores on their udders, but did not appear to suffer otherwise. The milkmaids and barn workers developed sores on their hands and arms, like those of smallpox but fewer in number; otherwise they were only mildly sick. When they recovered from this mild illness, they were immune to smallpox, even in the midst of a plague.

Edward Jenner, a young English doctor, studied the problem of smallpox infection and decided to perform a bold experiment. He got permission to infect a young boy, James Phipps, with the cowpox material from the sore on the hand of a milkmaid. James became only slightly sick. Some weeks later, Dr. Jenner infected him with smallpox germs. The boy did not become sick with the disease; he had become immune. Thus, Dr. Edward Jenner and the boy James Phipps showed for the first time that the body could be protected against the invasion of germs through immunization. Cowpox, a cow disease that people can catch, was the key to protection from smallpox.

We now know that cows, being more resistant than people to smallpox germs, do not become as sick from them. The virus is weakened within the animals. Healthy young calves are now used to produce the vaccine. They are inoculated with smallpox virus, through scratches, and the weakened virus in the sores that develop is removed. This is the protective vaccine.

Children as young as six months are given the protection of smallpox vaccine and may be revaccinated just before they are ready to enter school. Most schools require a certificate of vaccination for admission. The disease is under control in this country, but health officers are on constant alert against the threat of an epidemic. A certificate of vaccination not more than three years old, issued by the World Health Organization, is required for entry into this country from foreign lands. The discovery of a single case of smallpox would send millions of people to doctors for revaccination.

Not so many years ago, a child's complaint of a sore throat, and the appearance of white patches there, caused the parents and the doctor to fear diphtheria, a serious, often fatal children's disease. The bacteria, the bacilli, of diphtheria grow mainly in the throat, and produce a very powerful toxin; and their growth produces a membrane in the throat that can interfere with breathing.

An antitoxin was developed that could be injected to render the toxin harmless; but, unfortunately, it did not remain effective in the body very long, nor could it prevent the disease. Antitoxin is still injected by a doctor for suspicious cases of sore throats. It gives immediate protection against the diphtheria toxin, while the doctor undertakes curative measures against the germs.

However, doctors rarely see a case of diphtheria in children today. This is because they have been protected against the invasion of these bacilli with diphtheria toxoid, made from the toxin by treating it with the chemical formalin. The toxin then loses its poisonous quality but still causes the body tissues to produce antibodies against the disease. These protective substances stay in the blood for a long time, and during this time the inoculated child remains immune.

Diphtheria antitoxin is obtained from the blood plasma of a healthy horse that has been injected with toxoid.

Another bacterium that produces a powerful toxin in the body is the tetanus bacillus. The poison attacks the nerves in the spinal cord and causes the muscles all over the body to contract. Because the muscles of the jaws become tightly contracted, rigid, tetanus is sometimes called lockjaw. Should the toxin cause the chest muscles to contract as strongly, and to remain contracted, breathing would stop.

Tetanus bacilli are given off in the intestinal wastes of animals. The bacilli are able to survive very unfavorable conditions by forming a protective, resistant cover about themselves. In this resting condition they are called spores. Tetanus spores are very widely dispersed. When they get into a body through a wound, they break out of their protective cover and become active again.

A deep puncture wound may not appear dangerous. There may be very little bleeding, and the opening may close quickly. But any deep wound caused by an unclean object—a dirty nail, a tool, a jagged piece of metal, or such —may have become infected with the dangerous tetanus bacilli.

Because children often get puncture wounds, and sometimes don't tell, it has been found important to protect them. An antitoxin, prepared in a horse, gives immediate, temporary protection. A toxoid, prepared by treating the toxin with formalin, gets the tissues of the child to produce antibodies.

Another disease of childhood, now happily controlled, is whooping cough. The bacilli are killed with formalin and then injected into the child's tissues, which produce antibodies.

Protection against the triple threat of diphtheria, tetanus, and whooping cough is given to babies in a combined shot, sparing the baby a few painful moments with a hypodermic needle. Three such shots, one month apart, are given during the first year of life.

One of the last of the great plagues of childhood—polio —has been conquered within your lifetime. The poliomyelitis (infantile paralysis) virus attacks the nerves in the spinal cord that control voluntary movements. Thousands used to be afflicted with the disease each year. Many recovered without crippling, but many others suffered paralyzed limbs; some lost the use of their breathing muscles and had to live encased in "iron lungs." The late President Franklin Delano Roosevelt, who contracted the disease as an adult, became paralyzed in both legs.

The development of a vaccine was difficult because the polio virus will live only in body tissues. In the case of smallpox, cows and calves were unwitting partners in the preparation of a vaccine; but no such lucky break occurred with polio. The first advance came when a scientist found a way of growing the virus in certain monkey kidney tissues.

The final breakthrough came only a few years ago,

when Dr. Jonas B. Salk prepared a vaccine by treating the germs with formalin. The virus became inactive but was still capable of causing the body tissues to produce antibodies.

The vaccine, which was widely and thoroughly tested, has now been given to millions of children and thousands of adults. In 1965 there were only fifty-eight cases of poliomyelitis reported in this country.

To ensure protection, three shots of polio vaccine are given. The second is given four to six weeks after the first; the third seven months after the second. The last two are the booster shots. Booster shots increase the protection provided by the original shot. Another vaccine, the Sabin vaccine, which uses a weakened virus, has also been developed and may be used instead of the Salk vaccine.

Parents once regarded measles as a necessary, not too serious, tribulation of childhood. Once the child had had the disease, he was immune to subsequent infections of it. Many parents therefore exposed their children to an infection so that they might "catch it and have it over with." But the disease was sometimes fatal, and it often affected the central nervous system.

Very recently a vaccine of attenuated (weakened) virus has been developed that promises to bring measles under control, as was done only a little earlier for poliomyelitis, and still earlier for the other diseases of which you read in this chapter, beginning with smallpox.

The treatment of disease by prevention is called preventive medicine. Dr. Jenner came upon it by chance. Dr.

Louis Pasteur established it as a science after he had proven that infectious diseases are caused by microorganisms which can be controlled, thereby preventing disease. He succeeded in preparing a vaccine against the virus that causes rabies, once a fatal disease transmitted by the bite of a rabid (mad) animal. This vaccine is prepared from the spinal cords of rabbits that have been infected with the virus.

How does this knowledge of vaccination and inoculation help you? The unpleasant scratches and jabs by needles that you endured as an infant and young child have enabled you to grow to your present age without suffering many serious and possibly crippling illnesses.

As you learned earlier, you cannot prevent the invasion of your body by infectious microorganisms. They are in your nose and throat at this moment. But when you are in good condition—well rested, well nourished, and well clothed—you are more likely to resist an infection from any of them.

The diseases of early childhood and of the pre-teen years are, in the main, infectious ones. The protection that you have had through immunizing serums and vaccines, and through the use of the curative powers of antibiotic drugs, have enabled you to reach your teen years as healthy girls and boys.

Two serious diseases, syphilis and gonorrhea, have become increasingly prevalent among teenagers, and threaten the health and well-being of many of them. They are called social diseases because they are invariably transmitted directly from person to person. They are called venereal diseases (VD) because they enter the body through the organs of reproduction.

Gonorrhea infects the organs of excretion—the bladder, ureters, and the urethra. Syphilis is a far more serious disease, for a number of reasons. Because it is a social disease, young people are often reluctant to seek the advice of a parent or even of a doctor. They may therefore neglect it until the disease has made serious inroads in the body. Because its more damaging effects are not immediately apparent, a victim may delay getting help. In its later stages the disease seriously damages the heart, the large blood vessels, and the brain. An infected pregnant woman may infect her unborn baby so that it may be born blind or otherwise deformed.

Both syphilis and gonorrhea can be readily cured, especially if the doctor is consulted promptly. But there are no preventive serums or vaccines. A teenager may, however, remain immune to these diseases by bringing to the boy-girl relationship a code of behavior that values the physical, mental, and emotional well-being of others, as well as of oneself; a code of behavior that values the controls and disciplines that enrich rather than degrade human relationships.

The science of medicine and the science of hygiene have made it possible for you to look forward to a longer life than that of past generations. And it will be a healthier one, with your intelligent cooperation.

:thirteen:
Better be safe than sorry

The home may not be the safe haven that we have believed it to be. Of the ten million accidents that resulted in injuries in one recent year, half of them—five million—occurred in homes. This is five times the number of highway accidents. In 1965 there were 28,500 fatal accidents in homes! This is living dangerously.

Falls are the most frequent home accidents. The resulting injury may be only a small cut or bruise, but it could also be a gash from the sharp edge of a piece of furniture. It may be a slight bump on the head, but it could also be a brain concussion from striking the hard stone tile floor in the bathroom. It could be a bad sprain or even a broken bone. All of these types of injuries have resulted from falls in homes.

You can help to prevent falls in your home by seeking

out the accident booby traps. Look for worn and torn places in carpets and other floor coverings; broken door saddles; wires of electric lamps extending into the room; brooms, mops, dust pans, and toys left about underfoot. These are common causes of tripping accidents. You may find others in your home.

Look next for places where one may slip: well waxed and polished floors; small rugs that skid underfoot; a wet bathroom floor; oil or grease on linoleum or tiles; a toy on wheels left about. Whether you slip or trip, the resulting injury may be serious.

Falls from heights are harder. How would you reach for something on high? Would you clamber up on narrow shelves; balance on shaky boxes piled on top of one another; perch on a rickety ladder? Even if the ladder is in good repair, it is a good safety rule to have someone stand by while one is on the upper steps.

The danger of falls in the home is greatly increased if one runs through the rooms or moves about the house in the dark, without adequate night lights. And a tear in the carpet or a toy left about is even more hazardous if it is on a stairway, especially if one does not have a firm grip on the handrail, or if the handrail itself is in bad repair.

Every home has hazards that cause falling accidents. Find those in your home and make a family project of correcting them.

The kitchen is the most dangerous room in the home. Burns, ranking second to falls as home accidents, occur most frequently in the kitchen. You can be helpful in checking the danger points. Start at the cooking range.

If it uses gas it most likely has pilot lights to ignite the fuel at the burners. This does away with one hazard, matches. However, if the oven does *not* have a pilot light, you should know the safe way to light the gas. Light a match first and hold it at the opening through which the gas is ignited. Then turn on the gas for the oven. Doing it this way will prevent an explosion, and possible serious burns. Gas heaters, used in many homes, should also be lit in this way.

Are the handles of pots on the stove top turned so that they cannot be jostled as one passes? Pots with boiling liquids may be overturned in this way. Are there pot holders at hand with which to carry hot kettles or plates? Tripping or slipping while carrying either is a double accident hazard.

Scalding burns come from hot liquids or steam. Most often such injuries result from the accidental overturning of a pot, a plate, or a cup of very hot liquid. But sometimes burns are caused by a jet of steam from a kettle or a faulty radiator valve. In the bathroom very hot water may suddenly spurt from a faucet or shower head. The water should be mixed to the desired temperature before one enters the tub or shower.

Electrical burns may be very deep, because the spark is extremely hot. In removing a plug from a socket, the body of the plug should be pulled, not the wire. Frayed wires should be replaced. You may get a shock if you handle exposed wires, a defectively wired plug, or a metal electrical fixture with loose, broken, or defective wiring. If you handle it while you're in a bath, it may be fatal. Your wet body becomes a conductor and you may be electrocuted.

Objects with sharp cutting edges or with sharp points are another potential cause of accidents. Knives, forks, scissors, and picks can be dangerous weapons when they are used carelessly in the home. Each should be used only for the purpose for which it is intended. Thus, a knife should not be used to pry open a jar or a can; a fork should not be used as a pointer. Be sure you know how to use a sharp or pointed tool before you do so.

A jagged piece of broken glass can inflict a cruel cut. Hold a water glass or a glass jar firmly; but if it should slip from your hand, do not grab for it. You may catch it just as it shatters. Doors with glass panels should be opened and closed by using the doorknob. If they are of the swing type, the plate on the door frame should be pushed. Pushing on the glass panes is dangerous. They may break.

Pattering in your bare feet across a floor can be pleasant if there are no tacks, nails, slivers of glass, or other sharp objects on it. Wounds from them may not appear serious, but they may cause a tetanus infection.

The accident hazards of which you have just read are samplings of the more common types. There are others that frequently result in fatalities: gas poisoning from leaky jets, or from those carelessly left partially or completely open, or from a heater in poor repair; suffocating in plastic bags; swallowing poisons from the medicine chest, or swallowing household cleaning fluids such as rubbing alcohol, ammonia, fabric cleaner, and others.

Make a careful survey of the accident hazards in your home. You will be amazed at how many there are. Every member of the family should be determined to remove them. Repairs should be made promptly; night lights should be placed at dangerous places; household cleaning chemicals should be kept in a safe closet, out of reach of small children; the medicine chest should be out of bounds for them.

It isn't possible to list every accident hazard; there is always the unexpected. Besides, accidents are caused by people, not by places and things. Everyone in the family must be safety-conscious. Safe behavior in the home must be made a habit. The principle should be: "An ounce of prevention is worth a pound of cure."

How safe are you in school? The several years just ahead of you in high school are quite hazardous ones. In one year there were close to half a million accidents in this age group, twice as many among boys as among girls. They occurred while boys and girls were going to or returning from school; while moving about in the building; while playing in the gymnasium or playground; while in the shops and laboratories; and even while in the classrooms. Accidents were fewer when the girls and boys were under supervision.

How safe are you in the street? Falls are commonplace. Tripping over broken walks and curbs, or slipping on snow and ice, wet iron gratings or plates, or even fruit skins are everyday occurrences. Such falls may result only in bruises, but they may cause sprains, broken bones, or torn muscles. You should be especially alert in bad weather. The principal accident hazard in the street is, of course, automobile traffic. Ninety million motor vehicles travel along the streets and roads of this country. There are almost one million motor vehicle accidents in an average year, and about nine to twelve thousand pedestrians are fatally injured each year. What are your chances of escaping this danger?

At twenty-five miles an hour, the common speed limit within a city, a car travels thirty-seven feet in a second. A girl or boy, walking briskly at two and a half miles an hour, goes about four and a half feet in the same time. The car moves eight times as fast as the girl or boy.

It would take the girl or boy about thirteen seconds to walk across a sixty-foot street. In that time the car would have traveled 480 feet. Could you, as a pedestrian, beat the car at the crossing?

Jaywalking (crossing in mid-block) is responsible for most pedestrian-car accidents. Your chances of safely crossing the street are greater at street intersections. Where there are traffic lights, cross when they are green. They are there for your protection. Even then, you should look to your left or right, as may be necessary, to watch out for cars that are making a turn. Since some motorists are impatient or inconsiderate, don't try to outguess them or outsmart them, and don't depend on their brakes. A car traveling only ten miles an hour would still move eighteen feet after the brakes were applied. At twenty-five miles an hour the car would move seventy-four feet before it would be stopped. A body of flesh and bones is no match for a moving steel body weighing several thousand pounds. Where there are no traffic lights, allow yourself a wide margin of safety.

When you ride in the family car, be sure to use the seat belt and the shoulder harness (if there is one), so that you will not be thrown forward if the car has to stop suddenly, or be thrown out of the car if there is a collision. You may be spared serious injury. When you are ready to drive a car it will be time for you to learn and practice the rules for safe driving—for your own safety as well as that of other drivers and of pedestrians. By that time cars will have had better safety features built into them, and road engineers will have designed safer roads. But the principal factor in traffic safety will always be the skill, thoughtfulness, and safety-mindedness of the driver of the motor vehicle.

Because play space in cities is limited, boys, especially, often use the streets for their games. This is, of course, hazardous. Schoolyards, playgrounds, and play streets are much safer.

Skaters and riders of skate-scooters and bicycles use the streets at their peril. Unsteadiness, inability to stop short, or lack of alertness may result in a collision with a car. Thrown into the street, they may find themselves in the path of another, approaching car. The schoolyard, the playground, the play street, and the road in the park set aside for bicyclists are safer than the streets.

Accident hazards abound everywhere—in every activity, in every environment. Accidents are the fourth principal cause of death in all age groups; the principal cause for young people to the age of twenty-five; the cause of almost half of the deaths in your age group. Safety engineers and doctors believe that 90 percent of them may be prevented. Some people try to do so by wearing lucky charms, such as a rabbit's foot, or medals to ward off accidents. But since accidents are caused by people, a better way for you to prevent accidents is to be alert.

You can be very helpful to someone who has had a serious accident injury if you are prepared to give, or to assist in giving, first aid until a doctor comes. You can become first a junior, later a fully qualified, first aider by getting instruction and practice from The American Red Cross or the Scouts. Girls may learn first aid in a course in home nursing.

You will read here, briefly, how to treat the more common injuries. A first-aid manual will describe these treatments more fully and will include the treatments for other injuries.

If there has been a serious accident, the first aider will send for a doctor at once. Then he will immediately check the injured person's breathing and bleeding. Cessation of breathing for more than three minutes, or excessive bleeding, may be fatal. He will not move the victim unless it is necessary to prevent further, more serious, injury (for example, removing the victim of an automobile accident from a car that may burn or explode).

Useful first aid techniques

Arm splint and triangular bandage

Controlling bleeding by hand pressure and tourniquet

Any person who has been seriously injured will most likely have gone into shock. His skin will be pale, cold, and clammy; his breathing will be rapid or irregular, his pulse fast; and he will be frightened.

The first aider should always have the victim lie down, usually with his head lower than his feet. Then the injured person should be lightly covered, not so warmly as to cause sweating, and his clothing should be loosened. If his head or chest have been injured, the head and shoulders should be raised a little higher than the feet, but lowered again if he has any difficulty breathing. Most important, the first aider will remain calm; he must not panic.

If the victim's chest shows no breathing movements, breathing by artificial respiration must be started promptly. The mouth-to-mouth method is now preferred. The victim is placed on his back, and his mouth is opened and cleared with a finger. The head is tilted back by using one hand behind the neck and the other on top of the head. This hand is used also to keep the nostrils closed. If the victim is an adult, the first aider's mouth is placed over, and about, that of the victim, and air is blown into it every five seconds. For a child, the first aider's mouth covers both the mouth and the nose of the victim, and air is

Artificial respiration;
mouth to mouth method

Removing a victim from a live wire

blown in every three seconds. In between blowing, the victim's chest is watched for breathing movements.

If there are no breathing movements after a few minutes, the victim is turned on a side and slapped sharply between the shoulders. This is to dislodge any object in the throat that may be blocking breathing. Artificial respiration is resumed, and continued for a long time. It may take several hours before natural breathing can be restored.

Bleeding from a small cut or wound is readily controlled. The wound must, however, be protected from infection (invasion by germs). The wound should be washed in running water, then painted with an antiseptic. After that it should be covered with a sterile bandage—a sterile gauze pad that is held with a strip of adhesive tape. A clot will form, and the bleeding will have been stopped. Later, a scab will form.

If the wound is large and the bleeding severe, it will be more difficult to control. There isn't too much danger of immediate infection since the flow of blood will wash out any bacteria that may get into the wound. The doctor will take care of infection; the first aider must try to control the bleeding.

A large wad of sterile gauze or of clean rags (if the gauze is not available) should be pressed on the wound. If this compress becomes soaked with blood, another should be pressed on top of it. A third may have to be added to slow or stop the flow of blood. If it succeeds, the compress should be held in place with a thick, tight bandage until the doctor comes.

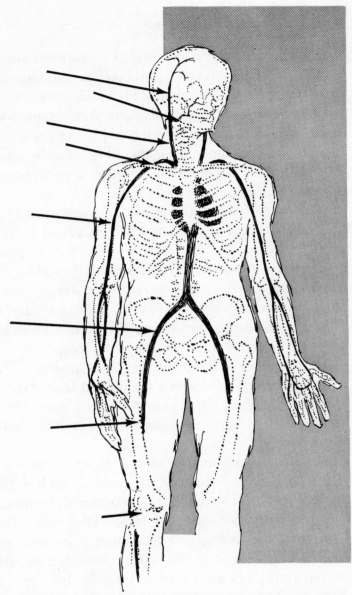

Arterial pressure points. Places where pressure may be applied to control bleeding in serious injuries

If the injury is on a limb, and the compress cannot control the bleeding, you may put direct pressure on an artery with your hand. The points to which pressure may be applied are shown on the diagram. A tourniquet—a band about a limb that can be tightened by twisting—may be used to stop bleeding, but it should be done by an expert. If a tourniquet is improperly applied, it may stop all circulation to the lower end of a limb.

The doctor will clean the wound, close it, and bandage it. He will inject tetanus antitoxin or toxoid if he thinks it necessary.

Burns are caused by overexposure to the sun, or by coming in contact with a hot object, hot water, or steam, or a flame, or an electric spark. Strong acids or alkalies such as lye may cause chemical burns. Burns may be mild (first degree) or severe (second and third degree).

A mild burn reddens the skin and "smarts". The pain may be relieved by washing the burned area in cold water for a few minutes, then coating it lightly with mineral oil, cold cream, or burn ointment. The effects of a mild burn pass quickly.

A more severe burn produces blisters. Unless it interferes with normal activity, or may be broken by such activity, a blister should not be punctured. It protects the delicate dermis beneath it while new epidermis is forming. If it should be necessary to drain a blister it should be done with a sterile needle, one whose point has been heated red in a match or gas flame. After it has been drained the area should be protected with a sterile gauze bandage to prevent infection.

Second degree burns may also be treated with mineral oil, cold cream, burn ointment, or burn-treatment gauze may be applied.

When the clothing of an accident victim is aflame, the first concern is to put out the fire by smothering it with a blanket, rug, coat, or whatever may be at hand. If a live electric wire is the cause of the fire it should be removed with a long wooden pole or stick. If possible the burned clothing may be cut away, but it should not be pulled from the skin. The burned areas should be covered with several layers of sterile gauze if it is available, or with clean, washed sheeting or towels. Someone would, meantime, have called a doctor.

If a strong acid or alkali has splashed on the hands or face, or in the eye, it should be washed with quantities of cold water to dilute it. On the skin baking soda may then be applied to an acid burn, vinegar to an alkali burn. Only water should be used in the eye until a doctor is seen.

Broken bones are common accident injuries. Limb bones are the most frequently broken, but fractures of the ribs, vertebrae, hips, and skull are not uncommon.

If after a collision or fall the victim's limb appears out of shape, or if he cannot move it, or cannot move part of it, you may suspect a break. The victim should not be moved until the injured limb has been supported so that it cannot move. This is done with a splint. The leg is wrapped with a pillow, a blanket, or a folded coat, and a stout stick or narrow board is laid alongside it. All are bound together, not too tightly, to make a rigid support. If an edge of the broken bone has pierced the skin and the wound bleeds, this will have to be controlled first, and the wound covered with a sterile gauze pack.

If the victim has pain in the neck or back, and if one or more limbs are paralyzed, you may suspect broken vertebrae of the neck or back. Such a victim must not be moved lest serious injury be done to the spinal cord. He should be made as comfortable as possible until expert aid arrives.

If the victim appears dizzy, or dazed, or is unconscious; and if blood oozes from the mouth, nose, or ears, you may suspect a brain concussion or a skull fracture. Keep him lying flat and quiet, lightly covered for warmth, and don't move him.

A bad sprain at a joint is treated by a first aider like a break, by splinting, so that the joint cannot be moved. It is often difficult to tell a sprain from a break until the joint is X-rayed.

Poisons are sometimes swallowed by adults through carelessness, by children through ignorance. If they are in their original containers, such substances are plainly labeled POISON, and instructions are given for first-aid treatment until the doctor comes. In general, the idea is to dilute the poison in the stomach (make it weaker), then get the victim to vomit it by placing a finger in the throat. Several glasses of water or of milk may be given. However, this treatment should not be used if there are any burns about the victim's mouth.

Some poisons require specific antidotes, substances that will make them harmless. This information is given on the label. When the doctor is called he should be told what poison was taken, if it is known.

These pages on first aid have been included so that you may understand and appreciate how helpful a first aider can be when there has been an accident, in the home or outside of it. You may want to become a qualified first aider through instruction with practice. And you now know how important it is to have a good first-aid manual at home and in the family car; and a good first-aid kit in both places.

The first-aid kit should be separate from the medicine chest, so that the supplies may be gotten at readily. Here is a check list for the car:

a packet of sterile gauze dressings, 4 by 4 inches

several rolls of gauze bandages, two inches wide

a roll of adhesive tape, one inch wide

a box of Band-Aids

a small bottle of antiseptic

a tube of vaseline

a pair of scissors

a pair of tweezers

a triangular bandage

a pair of twelve-inch splints

a blanket

Except for the blanket, of course, all the supplies will fit into a plastic or metal box. They should be replaced immediately after any of them are used.

For the home kit include all of the above, and add:

an eye cup

a medicine dropper

an ice bag

a hot water bottle or heating pad

an ear syringe

a mouth thermometer

a rectal thermometer
(for children)

a packet of sterile
swabs

a pint bottle of sterile salt
solution (a level teaspoon
to a pint of boiled water)

a half-pint bottle of boric
acid solution

a box of baking soda

Your parents may want to include in the medicine chest a few reliable remedies that they have found from experience to be useful in an emergency. And in the medicine chest at home, and in the first-aid kit in the car, you should have the telephone number of your doctor.

:fourteen:
Important teenage health decisions

Even in your pre-teen years you have begun to make decisions about how you live, sometimes guided by your parents, sometimes encouraged by them, and sometimes against their advice. The decisions may concern the kind of clothes you wear, the kind of television programs you watch, the friends you choose. During your teen years you will have to make a number of decisions in other areas that could affect your health throughout your life. In discussing these areas, we will be concerned only with their relationship to your physical and mental health, and not with the many moral attitudes that different people hold toward them.

Perhaps the first of these decisions will be whether to smoke or not to smoke. There will probably be a number of strong influences on you which could encourage you to start smoking. Other girls and boys of your age group may smoke, your parents may smoke, and you will be aware of the flood of cigarette advertising on television and in magazines. At this point, you are not a smoker, so your body has no craving; nor have you adopted a habit that is extremely difficult to break. Your only valid reason for wanting to start smoking is that other people smoke.

There are many negative angles to consider on the subject of smoking. The cost of cigarettes, for one thing, will make a considerable dent in your allowance—possibly more than you realize. More important is the fact that many household fires are started by careless smokers who go to bed with lighted cigarettes.

But the urgent reason for not smoking is that it is a serious health hazard. The nicotine in tobacco is a habit-forming drug. It can be a deadly drug in large doses, although the amount in a single cigarette is not injurious to most people. However, in some diseases of the blood vessels the nicotine in cigarettes may have a very damaging effect. And the drug is injurious to hearts that have already been damaged.

Tobacco smoke pollutes the air that we breathe, as we learned earlier, and pollutes the air in the lungs of the smoker even more. The smoke also contains irritants that affect the mouth and gums and the throats of heavy smokers, giving them husky, hoarse voices.

The health hazard from smoking that should especially impress you, though, is the relation of smoking to cancer, particularly lung cancer. Public health organizations in this country and in England, and the Office of the Surgeon

General of the United States Public Health Service have presented clear evidence that smokers are more likely to develop this disease than are non-smokers, and heavy smokers more likely than light smokers. These organizations also found that lung-cancer cases have increased as cigarette smoking has increased.

You will find on each package of cigarettes, and on each carton, this statement: "Caution. Cigarette smoking may be hazardous to your health." The warning has been placed there by an act of the Congress of the United States, for your protection.

Of course, lung cancer develops later in life. But the smoking habit is acquired early, most often in the teens, and sometimes even in the pre-teen years. You would be wise to make the decision now to refrain from smoking.

Another important decision that teenagers must make regarding health, especially in the upper teens, relates to the use of alcohol as a beverage. Many young people drink for the same reasons that they smoke—because others do.

Under the influence of alcohol, a shy person may talk more freely after one drink; after a number of them he may prattle foolishly. A timid person may become bolder after one drink; after a number of them he may become silly or belligerent. Such behavior is understandable when you know how alcohol affects the brain. The alcohol is quickly absorbed into the blood stream, and soon circulates through the brain. Here the alcohol is absorbed by the neurons of the nerve centers, diminishing their controls and impairing their work. The senses become less keen;

muscles do not coordinate as well; reactions to environmental conditions are slower; judgment is impaired. The more alcohol one drinks, the more noticeable the effects.

When a chemical causes cells to diminish their activity, it is called a depressant. A stimulant increases cell activity. What appears to be the stimulating effect of alcohol really results from its depressing effect on the nerve centers.

Most fatal automobile accidents are caused by drivers, both adult and teenage, whose vision, muscular coordination, reactions, and judgment have been impaired as a result of drinking alcohol—though not necessarily to the point of drunkenness.

Alcohol is particularly damaging to developing nervous systems. Moreover, normal body growth and development may be retarded when alcohol is substituted for nutritious foods and vitamins.

Some young people may boast about their ability to "hold their liquor." They are referring to the amount of alcohol that they can consume without getting drunk. These young people are really tempting fate, in this case alcoholism. Many a person starts out to be a social drinker, taking just one or two drinks for relaxation or stimulation, only to discover that he cannot control his thirst for liquor.

Alcoholism is a serious disease and makes one incapable of functioning effectively physically, mentally, or emotionally. The patient can sometimes give it up if he has the will to cooperate, but true alcoholism is incurable. The alcoholic who stops drinking is still an alcoholic—but a non-drinking alcoholic. It would never be safe for him to drink again.

To drink or not to drink? You should not drink at all, of course, until your nervous system has fully matured; and until you have informed yourself of the health hazards that are involved in your decision.

A third important decision for health that teenagers must make relates to their "experiments" with certain drugs, whether it be "just for kicks," or for other reasons.

The most serious health menace from drugs comes from the use of heroin, a narcotic. Doctors use a related drug, morphine (both are derived from opium), to alleviate severe pain or to induce sleep. The narcotic acts upon the cells in the forepart of the cerebrum as a depressant, to diminish conscious activity. But doctors use narcotics with great caution, for they are habit forming. That is, one may acquire an irresistible craving for repeated doses as the body cells develop a need for the drug. This is addiction. Heroin addiction is the most serious health hazard, and its use is unlawful.

While he is under the influence of heroin, the addict is free from the cares and worries of everyday living. His dream world may even be a very pleasant one. But when the effect of the narcotic wears off, the addict faces the problem of getting the next "fix" (dose). Because the distribution of heroin is illegal, the price is high, and addicts often resort to crime to get the money for it.

Drug addicts are sick people—physically, mentally, and emotionally. The sickness can be treated, and sometimes, with difficulty, it can be cured. However, only a small number of victims apply for and receive treatment. And many of those who are cured eventually slip back into

184 § Your Health and You

addiction. The temptation is strong, and the will is weak.

Then there are the "mind drugs." They affect the neurons of the cerebrum in different ways. Some are pep pills that increase cerebral activity, even when the mind has tired. Others are pacifiers, tranquilizers, that quiet down the overactive brain.

Some mind drugs produce hallucinations, unreal experiences of the mind. Such experiences may be pleasant, or fantastic, or horrible. The most readily available of such drugs is marijuana, which is smoked in a cigarette. The marijuana fumes are inhaled, absorbed into the blood, and carried to the brain. This drug does not result in addiction in the way that heroin does, but its use is a way of escape from reality, from facing the problems of everyday life.

A more potent hallucinatory drug is LSD. In the hands of competent doctors, LSD has been used in treating mentally disturbed people, and in studying how the mind works. Taken without the supervision of trained medical research workers, the drug may have, and has had, disastrous effects on the minds and personalities of the users.

Young people, ignorant of the actual dangers of drugs, may experiment with narcotics or with mind drugs because they don't want to appear "chicken" or because they are curious. The beginner is always sure that he will be able to quit when and if he wants to do so. That is how he is "hooked"; he finds that he cannot break off as easily as he thought he could.

You will probably have opportunities to experiment with narcotics and mind drugs in your teen years. You may be told convincing stories of their harmlessness. You would be wise to start learning everything you can about them now—from reading, from your parents, and from your physician. For no matter what some of your friends may say, your decision about experimenting with drugs is not one to be taken lightly.

You have read about the remarkable organization that is you. Trillions of cell units, organized into tissues, organs, and systems work in cooperation to carry on the activities inherent in your being alive.

A normal girl or boy inherits a body organization that is capable of performing its functions effectively. These functions are of two kinds: the physical activities that include digestion, respiration, circulation, excretion, motion; and the mental and emotional activities.

Normal cell activity may be impaired as a result of an invasion of the body by germs, or as a result of neglect or abuse of an organ or organs. Such impairment is recognized as disease by most people. Malfunction of the mind and of the personality is not always recognized and accepted as disease, although it is as real as any physical disease. As we have learned, a mental illness may contribute to a physical illness; and it can also work the other way around.

You function as a whole person, a unit. Good health is, therefore, a state of well-being that results when your physical and mental and emotional activities function properly. With an understanding and appreciation of this fact, you will more surely enjoy good health now and throughout your life.

A sound and effective personal health program must be

based on a knowledge of the organization of the body, of the role of each part in maintaining the unity of the whole; on an understanding of the interrelationship between you and your environment, including the people in it; on an appreciation of the importance of the mind in total health. You have read such information in this book.

The rules for healthful living that we have included are in accord with such knowledge, understanding and appreciation, and with current theory and practice in medicine and hygiene. However, good health does not result from information, but rather from its application and use. This book is your guide to healthful living; you must be the practitioner.

Books for further reading

American National Red Cross. *First Aid Textbook,* rev. ed. New York: Doubleday & Company, 1957.

Asimov, Isaac. *The Living River.* New York: Abelard-Schuman, Limited, 1959.

Asimov, Isaac. *The Human Brain.* Boston: Houghton Mifflin Company, 1963.

Carlson, Anton J. *Machinery of the Body.* Chicago: University of Chicago Press, 1961.

Diehl, Harold S. *Healthful Living,* 7th ed. New York: McGraw-Hill Book Company, 1964.

Frohse, Franz. *Atlas of Human Anatomy,* 6th rev. ed. New York: Barnes & Noble, 1961.

Gramet, Charles. *Light and Sight.* New York: Abelard-Schuman, Limited, 1963.

Gramet, Charles. *Sound and Hearing.* New York: Abelard-Schuman, Limited, 1965.

Guyton, Arthur C. *Function of the Human Body,* 2nd ed. Philadelphia: W. B. Saunders Co., 1964.

Irwin, Leslie W. *Health for Better Living.* Columbus: Charles E. Merrill Books, 1964.

Kilander, Holger F. *Health for Modern Living,* 2nd ed. Englewood Cliffs: Prentice-Hall, 1965.

Miller, Benjamin F. *Man and His Body.* New York: Simon and Schuster, 1960.

Rogers, Terence A. *Elementary Human Physiology.* New York: John Wiley & Sons, 1961.

Schifferes, Justus J. *Healthier Living,* 2nd ed. New York: John Wiley and Sons, 1965.

Strasser, Marland K. *Fundamentals of Safety Education.* New York: The Macmillan Co., 1964.

Index